● Browsing the Book Stalls ●

THIS REVIEW CONCERNED
THE FIRST EDITION

**HOW TO BE A MUSIC PUBLISHER;
by Walter E. Hurst & Don Rico; Seven
Arts Press Inc.; 125 pages (paperback);
$10.**

The authors, a top Hollywood music attorney and a leading artist/illustrator and writer, have collaborated to produce a primer which covers the main principles of the music publishing business for songwriters, artists, musicians, distributors, teachers, students, accountants, attorneys, publicists and anyone else seeking to understand the rudiments of this multimillion-dollar industry.

While it is by no means a comprehensive guide to this end of the music business (and anyone seeking to enter it would be well advised to use this book merely as a point of departure for further research), nevertheless it does manage to provide a good overflow of the fundamentals which must be mastered.

It covers some of the basics of copyright law, contracts, licensing agreements, acquiring and selling song rights, etc. It also covers key principles of musical composition. It is an excellent companion volume to Hurst's earlier work (with William Storm Hale): "Introduction to Music/Record Copyright, Contracts and Other Business and Law."

There is much to learn about the business and legal aspects of the music and record industry — and this book is a welcome addition to available books on these subjects. **— John Charnay**

Library of Congress Cataloging in Publication Data

Hurst, Walter E
    How to be a music publisher.

    (Entertainment industry series ; v. 11 ISSN 0071-0695)
    "A 7 Arts Press entertainment industry book."
    Includes index.
    1. Music--Publishing--United States. 2. Music
trade. I. Rico, Donato, joint author. II. Title.
III. Series: Hurst, Walter E. Entertainment industry
series ; v. 11.
ML3790.H89   338.4'7'7840973   79-15268
ISBN 0-911370-35-8
ISBN 0-911370-36-6 pbk.

i

BOOKS BY THE AUTHOR(S):

H=Hardcover, P=Paperback

1. The Record Industry Book (7th edition) H $15.00, P $10.00
2. The Music Industry Book H $25.00
3. The Publisher's Office Manual H $25.00
4. The U.S. Master Producers & British Music Scene Book H $25.00
5. The Movie Industry Book H $35.00
6. The Managers, Entertainers and Agents Book H $35.00
7. Film/TV Law (Your Introduction To Film/TV Copyright, Contracts and Other Law) H $15.00, P $10.00
8. Film Superlist: 20,000 Motion Pictures in the Unites States Public Domain H $95.00, P $59.50
9. Music/Record Business and Law (Your Introduction To Music/Record Copyright, Contracts and Other Business and Law) H $15.00, P $10.00
10. Motion Picture Distribution (Business and/or Racket?) H $15.00, P $10.00
11. How To Be A Music Publisher H $15.00, P $10.00
12. Your Income Tax Comic Book P $10.00
13. How To Start A Record Or Independent Production Company (Pending)
14. How To Register A Trademark (Pending)
15. © COPYRIGHT H $15.00, P $10.00
16. COPYRIGHT REGISTRATION   Forms PA & SR   HOW TO...

WARNING - It is quite possible that:

1. There may be errors in this book;
2. You may interpret something in this book differently from the way we mean it;
3. Something which was correct when this book was written is not correct at the time you read it;
4. The law may change after we write this book.
5. Future editions may contain corrections, if we have learned of errors.

a 7 Arts Press Entertainment Industry Book

HOW TO BE A MUSIC PUBLISHER

By

WALTER E. HURST

&

DON RICO

The Ins and outs of the MUSIC PUBLISHING BUSINESS for: SONGWRITERS, ARTISTS, MUSICIANS, DISTRIBUTORS, TEACHERS, STUDENTS, ACCOUNTANTS, ATTORNEYS, PUBLICISTS

ISSN 0071-0695 The Entertainment Industry
              Series. Volume 11.
ISBN 0-911370-35-8 Hardcover $15.00
ISBN 0-911370-36-6 Paperback $10.00
   *For copies of this or our other books, please
   send money to:*
SEVEN ARTS PRESS, INC.
PO. BOX 649, HOLLYWOOD, CALIFORNIA 90028

*"Every man who knows how to read has it in his
power to magnify himself...."*
                              Aldous Huxley

Magnify yourself by reading all of the books in
THE ENTERTAINMENT INDUSTRY SERIES.

INVATION TO READERS AND COLLECTORS

Matthew Gentry

When I wanted to learn how to be a music publisher, <u>I asked</u> a lot of questions. <u>Some people were courteous</u>, and took a little time to speak to me about acquiring songs, performing paperwork, trying to get a record, and they <u>recommended</u> that I read HOW TO BE A MUSIC PUBLISHER and the other books of the *7 ARTS PRESS "ENTERTAINMENT INDUSTRY SERIES."*

Other people in the Entertainment Industry knew a little about their respective jobs (musician, producer, engineer, booking agent), *thought that music publishing was potentially tremendously lucrative*, *admitted their ignorance* about fictitious names, joining a performing rights society, activities of the Copyright Office, etc., and then <u>recommended</u> that I read HOW TO BE A MUSIC PUBLISHER.

The out of print first edition concerned activities under the Copyright Act of 1909, as amended.

The Copyright Act of 1976, which was generally effective as of January 1, 1978, made the first edition a valuable, historically, and partially obsolete edition of *HOW TO BE A MUSIC PUBLISHER*.

This is the <u>New</u> second edition.

The text has been wholly rewritten for this new second edition of *HOW TO BE A MUSIC PUBLISHER*.

I have read the first draft of this edition of *HOW TO BE A MUSIC PUBLISHER*.

I work with and for many music publishers, some of whom waste time and money because they don't understand the basics set forth in *HOW TO BE A MUSIC PUBLISHER*.

I teach my publisher clients, and when people ask me How To Be A Music Publisher, I try to be courteous. But my time is too short and too expensive to answer everyone, so it is my turn to highly recommend that people read HOW TO BE A MUSIC PUBLISHER.

TABLE OF CONTENTS

CHAPTER NO: PAGE

      Invitation To Readers And Collectors   v

1.   Come Into My Publisher's World   1.

2.   I Want To Be A Music Publisher   2.

3.   Talent   3.

4.   Time   5.

5.   Money   8.

6.   Contacts   12.

7.   Knowledge   16.

8.   ASCAP, BMI, SESAC   20.

9.   Joining ASCAP, BMI, SESAC   22.

10.   Fictitious Name Certificate   23.

11.   U.S. Employer Identification Number   25.

12.   Employees   26.

13.   Payroll Problems & Procedures   27.

14.   The Songwriter - Needed Information.   29.

15.   Songwriter's Information Sheet   30.

16.   Songwriter's List of Songs.   31.

17.   Songwriter's Royalty Summary   32.

18.   Don't Overpay Your Songwriter
       (The Publisher As A Pigeon)   33.

19.   The Publisher Is In The Money Business   35.

20.   Uncle Sam Is In The Taxing Business   37.

21.   The Song Pink Label File Folder   39.

22.   The Lead Sheet File Folder   41.

23.   ANSCR-The Alpha-Numeric System For
       Classification of Recordings.   42.

24.   Which Song Is On Which Record?   44.

25.   Costs Of Copies And Files   46.

26.   Income From Hits And Non Hits.   47.

27.   Copyright Office Forms   48.

28.   Request Letter To Copyright Office   50.

29.   Search Letter to Copyright Office   51.

30.   Registration Letter of Transmittal.   52.

31.   The Publisher's Green Label Copyright
       Office Files   53.

32.   The Publisher's Green Label Ascap Files   56.

33.   The Publisher's Green Label BMI Files   57.

      ASCAP, BMI, COPYRIGHT OFFICE FORMS   58
      DON RICO'S ILLUSTRATIONS   63
      INDEX   75

CHAPTER 1. COME INTO MY PUBLISHERS WORLD.

I am an attorney.

I do a lot of work in the entertainment industry.

Many clients want to start music publishing companies.

Sometimes I ask clients to read HOW TO BE A MUSIC PUBLISHER _before_ the office conference (so that they may more easily understand what I have to say.)

Sometimes, _after_ an office conference, I ask clients to read HOW TO BE A MUSIC PUBLISHER (so that they may reinforce their recollections and understandings)

The odds are high, that most readers of this book and I will never meet.

Therefore, I have tried to include in this book both part of my diaglogue with and answers to the clients' questions.

I am not blessed with musical ability.

I hope that you, who are more blessed in musical ability than I am, will be able to enrich your time, careers and pocketbooks by using the information contained in this book.

If you are talented in business, office procedures, paperwork, then you may be able to enjoy a better career in the music industry than many musically talented people.

Many a musician has been suprised to learn how much of the music industry has nothing to do with playing music.

Knowing the worth of yourself and your music monetarily is very important.

CHAPTER TWO. I WANT TO BE A MUSIC PUBLISHER!

Good for you!

Possibly, music publishing is the best *bet* in *risky* show business, filled with pitfalls.

You have to combine:

1. *Talent*
2. *Time*
3. *Money*
4. *Contacts*
5. *Knowledge*

TALENT is required to:

1. *Obtain rights in songs.*
2. *Merchandise the songs.*
3. *Complete necessary paperwork*
4. *License and assign rights in songs.*

TIME is required to:

1. *Obtain rights in songs.*
2. *Merchandise the songs.*
3. *Complete necessary paperwork*
4. *License and assign rights in songs.*

MONEY is required to:

1. *Obtain rights in songs (unless rights are received without any advance).*
2. *Merchandise the songs.*
3. *Complete necessary paperwork.*
4. *License and assign rights in songs.*

CONTACTS are required to:

1. *Obtain rights in songs.*
2. *Merchandise the songs.*
3. *Complete necessary paperwork.*
4. *License and assign rights in songs.*

KNOWLEDGE is required to:

1. Obtain rights in songs
2. Merchandise the songs
3. Complete necessary paperwork.
4. License and assign rights in songs.

CHAPTER 3.   TALENT

TALENT is required to:

1. *Obtain rights in songs*
2. *Merchandise songs*
3. *Complete necessary paperwork*
4. *License and assign rights in songs.*

Beauty, I have been told, is in the eyes of the beholder.

I am a lawyer and I behold songs, as a Lawyer.

I see a song as a "Creative Work" and I see "Ownership" rights in a song.

I see a songwriter, as a *manufacturer* of a song.

I see a manufacturer (the songwriter) having rights in the product manufactured (the song).

The songwriter may assign his rights to anyone selected by the songwriter.

Also, the songwriter may decide to keep all of his rights.

The songwriter may decide to become a music publisher.

A music publisher may obtain rights in songs, which the songwriter publisher wrote, and rights in songs which were written by other songwriters.

A publisher, who wants to obtain all rights in a song from a songwriter, must have talent of persuasion.

That talent may consist of:
ONE: <u>persuading</u> the songwriter to sign a contract.

TWO: <u>Merchandising</u> the song which may consist of a variety of talents. required to prepare:

a) *A lyric sheet.*
b) *A lead sheet.*
c) *An arrangement.*
d) *A demo recording.*
e) *A master recording.*

THREE: <u>Talent to know</u> and/or get a song to:

a) *Artists*
b) *Managers*
c) *Producers.*
d) *Record companies*
e) *Others who review and influence the selection of songs to be recorded.*
f) *Others who select songs for commercial exploitation in various media.*

g) *Radio stations*

h) *Other publicizers of recorded product, both singles and albums.*

FOUR: Talent <u>to complete paperwork</u> may include:

a) *Talent to know the <u>uses</u> of various contracts, forms, letters of transmittal, royalty statements, etc.*

b) *Talent to know the <u>contents</u> of various contracts, forms, letters of transmittal, royalty statements, etc.*

c) *Talent to <u>prepare</u> (by filling in blanks) various contracts, forms, letters of transmittal, royalty statements, etc., and make them binding.*

d) *Talent to transmit, file, find in files, various contracts, forms, letters of transmittal, royalty statements, etc.*

e) *Talent to read, write, type, photocopy.*

FIVE: Talent to <u>license and assign</u> rights in songs include:

a) *Talent to know when to use a variety of contract blanks for uses such as: co-publishing, royalty-sharing, mechanical-licenses, synchronization licenses, foreign publishing, etc.*

b) *Talent to negotiate the most favourable terms under a given circumstance.*

CHAPTER FOUR. TIME

TIME is required to:

1. *Obtain rights in songs.*
2. *Merchandise songs*
3. *Complete paperwork*
4. *License and assign rights in songs.*

1. Time is required *to obtain rights* in songs:

(a) Time is required to write lyrics and compose music and thus manufacture songs. The rights in the song are those of the creator or creators.

(b) Time is spent in trying to find co-writers of songs, in co-writing, in trying to agree to the shares of songwriting and publishing rights.

(c) Time is spent in talking with songwriters, in listening to songs, in negotiating contracts with songwriters.

(d) Time may be spent in considering whether the songwriter should be offered one or more of the following contracts:

    i.   *One-song contract.*
    ii.   *One-project work-for-hire contract.*
    iii. *Long-term non-exclusive contract*
    iv.   *Long-term exclusive contract.*

(e) Time may be spent acquiring money. Money may be obtained through:

    i.   *Earning it as a publisher.*
    ii.   *Earning it in other activities.*
    iii. *Borrowing it.*
    iv.   *Organizing a partnership or corporation.*

2. Time is required to merchandise songs.

(a) Time is required to determine which *merchandising* tools you want:

    i.   *Lyric sheets.*
    ii.   *Lead sheets.*
    iii. *Inexpensive demo recording.*
    iv.   *Expensive demo recording*
    v.   *Master recording.*

(b) Time is required to meet the people, who are prospectively useful to you, as customers for your rights (for example, record companies, which want the right to reproduce your song on records.)

(c)   Time is required to meet the people, who might be useful in other ways. (For example, a manager, who selects material to be recorded by an artist).

(d)   Time is required to bring your tools (lyric sheets, lead sheets, demo, master) to your prospective (record company, manager, etc)

(e)   Sometimes there is a conflict between the spending of money and the spending of time.

(f)   Should you use your own time (valued at so much per hour for the time required) or the time of a messenger (cost may be $10.) or a private or government carrier (cost may be $1.00)? (The U.S. Postal Service has a variety of services: 1st class mail, special delivery, express mail, etc.)

3.   *Time is spent to complete paperwork:*

(a)   Contract between two parties, a songwriter/(assignor) and a publisher/assignee, in which the songwriter *assigns* rights to a song and the publisher promises to pay royalties to the *assignor.*

(b)   Contract between a publisher and a record company, in which the publisher licenses *the record company to use the songs on records, and the record company promises to pay a royalty.* This is called a mechanical license.

(c)   Contract between a publisher and a sheet music company, in which the publisher licenses the sheet music company to use the song for sheet music, in song books, and for other printed uses, usually for royalties. (sometimes for flat fees).

(d)   Contract between a publisher and a television or motion picture company, in which the publisher licenses the use of the song in a television or motion picture production, usually for a flat fee. This is known as a synchronization license.

(e)   Registration form used by the publisher to inform a performing rights society that the song belongs to the publisher.

(f)   Registration form used by the publisher to inform the Register of Copyrights that the publisher claims the copyright of a song. Before 1978, publishers used Form E. Since January 1, 1978, publishers use Form PA.

(g)   Other Paperwork.

4.   *Time is required to license and assign rights in songs:*

(a)   There is a difference between a license and an assignment.

(b)   *ASSIGNMENT has been defined as:*
"A transfer or making over to another of the *whole* of any property..."
Black's Law Dictionary, 4th edition.

(c)   *LICENSE has been* defined *as:*

"Authority or liberty given to do or forbear any act."
Black's Law Dictionary, 4th edition.

(d)   The 1976 Copyright Act, in Section 101, defines a *"transfer of copyright ownership"* as *"an assignment, mortgage, exclusive license, or any* other conveyance, alienation or hypothecation of a copyright or of any of the exclusive rights comprised in a copyright, whether or not it is limited in time *or place of effect, but not including a nonexclusive license"*

(e)   License contracts should clearly show whether the contract is for an exclusive license or a nonexclusive license.

CHAPTER FIVE.   MONEY

Money is required to:

1.   *Obtain rights in songs (unless rights are received without any advance)*
2.   *Merchandise the songs.*
3.   *Complete necessary paperwork*
4.   *License and assign rights in songs.*

1.   Money is required to obtain rights in songs *(unless rights are received without any advance)*

(a)   *Many decades ago, it was quite customary for a songwriter to manufacture a song and to sell the manufactured song to a distributor, the publisher, for a flat fee.*

(b)   *The publisher would take his gamble by risking his time and money to make a song into a commercial hit.*

(c)   *Generally, the songwriter would make a profit, while the publisher would have a loss. (lucky songwriter.)*

(d)   *In those rarer instances, in which the song would become a hit, the publisher would be able to retain the profit without making additional royalty payments to the songwriter.   (lucky publisher)*

(e)   *Later, songwriters fought for the right to receive royalties.*

(f)   *The Songwriters Protection Association (S.P.A) prepared a form contract and urged members of the S.P.A to use only that contract.   S.P.A. also revised that contract.*

(g)   *The name of the Songwriters Protection Association was changed to American Guild of Authors and Composers. (A.G.A.C)*

(h)   *After passage of the 1976 Copyright Act, A.G.A.C again revised its form contract.*

(i)   *Many concepts contained in the A.G.A.C contract are also contained in other contracts, between songwriters and publishers.*

(j)   *Royalties, are set forth in varying detail in various contracts.   For example: Publisher shall pay to Songwriter:*
(a)   *50% of receipts, from record companies.*
(b)   *10% for every piano copy sold by publisher for more than $100.00*

(k)   *Contracts may offer a Songwriter both:*

(i)   *an advance against royalties*

(ii)   *royalties.*

2.   Money is required to merchandise the songs:

     (a) The least expensive merchandising tool may be the <u>lyric</u>
<u>sheet.</u> This may consist of a piece of paper, possibly 8½" X 11",
containing the song's title, name(s) of lyricist and composer,
legibly written or typed lyric, publisher's name, address, telephone
number, and a copyright notice.

     (b) A <u>lead sheet</u> is more expensive. It may be on easy-to-file
8½" X 11" paper or on more customary larger size paper, with many
staves for notes and spaces between staves for lyrics.   The
first page should show the song's title, music by_____,
lyrics by _____, the publishers name, address, telephone number
a copyright notice, and the name of the applicable performing
rights organization.

     (c) A <u>demo</u> may be on tape (reel and/or cassette) or disc.
It may be inexpensively produced or expensively produced. A "demo"
is supposed to <u>demon</u>strate the song.

     (d) A <u>master</u> may be on tape or disc. A publisher may
prepare a <u>master</u>.

     (e) Two basic differences between a "demo" and a "master"
are <u>commercial quality</u> and <u>rights clearances</u>.

     (f) "Commercial quality" is in the ears of the "beholder."

     (g) "Rights clearances" concern the rights to use the sound
recording on phonograph records, television or movie soundtrack
and other uses.

     (h) "Rights clearances" may concern copyright, right of
privacy, employer-employee relations.

3.   Money is required to complete necessary paperwork.

     (a) Many of the forms and form-contracts are simple to
complete. There are blanks for the title of the song, the
contributions (lyrics, music) of the songwriter(s), the respective
shares of the songwriter(s), the addresses, social security
numbers, performance rights society, and year of birth of the
songwriter(s), and:

     The name(s), address(es), performing rights society of the
publisher(s), the copyright notice.

     (b) Money is needed to acquire, forms, file forms, find
filed forms, fill out forms, forward forms to the other party,
and to follow through.

     (c) Sometimes, forms do not set forth the oral agreement
between the parties.

     (d) The parties may want to alter the forms with additions,
deletions, modifications.

(e) *The parties may believe that they have the ability to alter the forms, and do so.*

(f) *The parties may believe that they have the ability to alter forms, but may decide not to do so.*

(g) *The parties may prefer to remain on personal friendly relationship, and may prefer to do their negotiating fighting through representatives (agents, managers and lawyers.)*

(h) *Representatives may, or may not, reach agreements on alterations.*

(L) *Representatives if they are paid - can cost a lot of money.*

(m) *The cost of operating a music publishing business, also includes the cost of representatives.*

(n) *It pays for publishers to learn the publishing business, so that publishers utilize their representatives properly.*

(o) *Using representatives to prepare paperwork may be worthwhile depending on the circumstances.*

4. **Money is required to license and assign rights in songs.**

(a) *The preparation of individual or form contracts may be the task of the licensor, or licensee, assignor or assignee.*

(b) *Definitions and examples.*

(i) *Licensor* - One who grants permission (music publisher)

(ii) *Licensee* - One who receives permission (record company)

(iii) *Assignor* One who assigns rights (original publisher)

(iv) *Assignee* One who receives rights (United Kingdom sub-publisher).

(c) *Money is required to obtain information, concerning current industry practices.*

(d) *Such information is furnished at meetings of the California Copyright Conference, Association of Independent Music Publishers, Songwriters Resources Services, American Guild of Authors and Composers, alumni of San Francisco's College for Recording Arts, ASCAP, B.M. I. etc.*

(e) *Such information may be contained in music trade and fan publications such as Billboard, Radio and Records, Cash Box, Record World, Variety, Hollywood Reporter, International Musician, Overture, AFTRA's newsletter, Backstage.*

(f)   Such information may be known by persons, who are active in the industry, such as certain lawyers, managers agents, publishers, and money-conscious artists.

(g)   Assignments and Licenses concern:

     i   Scope which rights?
     ii   Duration of assignment, termination, reversion of rights.
     iii   Money amounts, as advances and as royalties.
     iv   Royalty statements due dates and rights to audit
     v   Consequences if assignee fails to pay.
     vi   Rights of assignee to re-assign.
     vii   Reservation of certain rights by original assignor in the territory of assignee
     viii   Territory

(h)   A foreign publisher may offer to pay a U.S. publisher one basic royalty: 50% of the gross receipts from all sources.

(i)   An English publisher, who has rights for the entire world outside the U.S. and Canada may grant a sub-publishing deal to a South American company for the territory of the Western Hemisphere, below the United States.

(j)   The South American publisher may grant a sub-publishing deal to a Mexican publisher for the territory of Mexico

(k)   If every deal provides for payment at 50% royalties then:

     (i)   The Mexican publisher may collect royalties of $10,000 and pay $5000 to the South American Publisher,

     (ii)   Who pays $2500 to the English Publisher,

     (iii)   Who pays $1250 to the U.S. Publisher

(1)   The royalties in Mexico may be royalties on sales in Mexico by a Mexican record company, which sells copies of a U.S. hit single or LP.

(m)   There are "collection deals", in which a foreign publisher pays a U.S. publisher 85%(or more) of the money collected by the foreign publisher from the foreign record company which sells the records containing the original hit recording.

(n)   For example, a Japanese sub-publisher, who collects royalties for eight songs on an LP may collect $10,000. He has the obligation of paying $9,500 to the American publisher.

(o)   Compare the $10,000 received by the Mexican publisher (the U.S. publisher received $1250) with the $10,000 received by the Japanese publisher (the U.S. publisher received $9500).

(p)   The difference in the amounts received lies in the language of the sub-publishing contracts, and the knowledge of the negotiators.

11.

CHAPTER 6. CONTACTS.

CONTACTS *are required to:*

1. *Obtain rights in songs*
2. *Merchandise the songs.*
3. *Complete necessary paperwork*
4. *License and assign rights in songs.*

xxx

1. Contracts are required to obtain rights in songs.

   (a) *The publisher's number one contact may be himself.*

   (b) *The publisher may be a songwriter. The songwriter, as manufacturer of the song, may decide that the best international distributor of the rights in the song is: Himself.*

   (c) *The publisher may also be an artist, or producer, or record company.*

   (d) *The publisher may decide that the proper artist to record the song first is: Himself.*

   (e) *Another contact of the songwriter may be a hit artist with a big ego or big greed or both.*

   (f) *Big artists with big egos may want to be recognized as songwriters.*

   (g) *Big name artists who are greedy may want to cut a share for themselves out of the songwriter's share and/or the publisher's share.*

   (h) *Songwriters and publishers are in the business of making money out of songs; sometimes it is better to wind up with a portion of the songwriting and publishing share of a song recorded by a big name artist, than to own all of the songwriting and publishing share of an unrecorded song.*

   (i) *Contacts may be listed in various columns:*

   Person, Position, Company, Powers, Artist influenced

   (j) *A publisher may make a target list of contacts, which he wants to make:*

   Company, Position, Name, How To Meet Him or Her

   (k) *Rights may be obtained from songwriters, original publishers, foreign publishers.*

2. Contacts are required to merchandise the song.

   (a)   The publisher may have the talent (personally or in other members of his organization)to prepare lyric sheets, lead sheets demos and masters.

   (b)   The production of sound recordings (demos and masters) requires a location (office, garage studio, commercial studio), equipment (recording, playback, editing), personnel (performing functions of producer, engineer, conductor, vocalist(s), musician(s)) tape (original recording, generations, copies).

   (c)   One way of merchandising a song is to prepare a whole package, consisting of:

> (i)   Songs
> (ii) An artist free to sign a long term recording contract.
> (iii) Masters sufficient for the initial release of a single or LP album.

   (d)   The publisher dons the hat of a producer, and signs an artist (solo, duo, group) to a long term contract.

   (e)   The publisher, as producer, personally or utilizing services of another producer, produces several masters.

   (f)   The publisher-producer should develop his contacts with recording studios to achieve the goals of recording in the studio he desires,at a cost which he can afford.

   (g)   Some recording studios allow "friends" to utilize the studio during unbooked time (such as weekends or from midnight to 8 AM) on very favorable terms (such as "nothing down and pay full rate card amounts if and when the project is sold to a record company.")

   (h)   Some union and non-union vocalists and musicians work on similar terms (such as "no pay now and pay full union scale when the session.is cleared with the union.")

3. Contacts are required to complete paperwork.

   (a)   There are "correct" ways of doing things, and there are ways of doing things, which are not quite "correct".

   (b)   Recording studios like to be paid cash in front or on purchase orders duly executed by swiftly paying,established companies.

   (c)   A recording studio may make an oral deal of "use the studio now, pay when the project is sold."

   (d)   The recording studio bookkeeping department may duly log all the time and other charges, enter the total on a ledger card containing the publisher/producer's account, and eventually bill the publisher.

   (e)   The person who worked for (or owned) the recording studio at the time the original oral deal was made, may be long gone,

or may deny the deal, if and when the recording studio bills the producer/publisher for payment in full.

(f)   It is important that at the time the original deal is made with the publisher's contact at the recording studio, that the paperwork, containing the oral deal provisions, be completed, and executed in front of witnesses.

(g)   This is only one example of the concept, "contacts are required to complete paperwork."

(h)   If you have an arrangement with the company represented by a contact, try to complete the paperwork before the contact leaves the company or becomes unfriendly.

4.   Contacts are required to license and assign rights in songs.

(a)   The record industry manufactures and sells records featuring new and established artist(s)

(b)   Record companies need masters for singles and LPs.

(c)   An artist's name sometimes serves as a "brand" name. Customers, whether for food appliances or records, tend to buy brand name products rather than products with which they are not familiar.

(d)   Buyers of records tend to look for releases by their favorite established artist.

(e)   Record Companies want a flow of releases of records featuring established artists.

(f)   Thus there is pressure on artists by record companies to record steadily.

(g)   The album output may be twice annually, or once a year, or once during January-August and once for the Christmas Season or it may be even more irregular.

(h)   Artists want to record for reasons of fun, hope, and dreams of a hit, to get rest from strenuous road trips and for money.

(i)   Record companies and artists need songs.

(j)   Sources of songs include the artist, the producer, other insiders connected with the session, and publishers, for whom these people (artist, producer, insider) are contacts.

(k)   One or more group members may have arrangements with publishers to administer publishing companies, owned by group member(s), or to co-publish with such group member(s). The administrative publisher handles or supervises promotion, selling, negotiation, legal, accounting, record keeping activities.

(l)   A publisher may be told by an artist "I will sing your song, only if you pay me a share of your receipts."

(m)   A publisher may seek an artist, who is willing to utilize a song, if the artist is given co-publishing.

(n)   A publisher must distinguish between a so-called "friend,"

14.

(who may be any acquaintance, other than an enemy), a "friend" to
have fun with, who may be an unreliable bum, or a friend-in-need
(who needs the publisher) and a friend indeed. (the friend who helps the
publisher),

   (o)   All these people, and others, are possible contacts.

   (p)   Your "cold-blooded" job is to figure out how to use your
contacts to your advantage.

   (q)   Your "warm-blooded job is to figure out how to benefit both
yourself and your contacts in your dealings.

CHAPTER 7.   KNOWLEDGE

KNOWLEDGE is required to

1. *Obtain rights in songs.*
2. *Merchandise the songs.*
3. *Complete necessary paperwork.*
4. *License and assign rights in songs, skillfully.*

X   X   X

1. *Knowledge is required to obtain rights in songs.*

(a)   *The publisher should know what he wants.*

(b)   *Does the publisher want to see just a select few songwriters?*
If a publisher sees ten songwriters an average one hour each per week,
then the publisher spends ten hours in the song acquisition portion of
his business. If a publisher has other activities, (inside or outside
the music industry), can the publisher afford to spend ten hours
weekly trying to acquire songs?

(c)   *Does the publisher want to sign a songwriter to a long term*
exclusive songwriting contract? There are advantages and disadvantages

(d)   *The publisher should know the advantages: the whole body of*
manufactured items (songs) which the manufacturer creates during
the duration of the contract, is dumped into the publisher's inventory.

(e)   *Processing songs into the publisher's inventory is time*
consuming and expensive:

(i)   *Preparing a list of songs and a receipt furnished to the*
songwriter, executed by both parties, is important.

(ii)   *Possibly preparing a one-song songwriter-publisher contract to*
cover each specific song.

(iii)   *Preparing a lyric sheet, lead sheet, demo, for each song.*

(iv)   *Registering the song with the Copyright Office, possibly on*
an individual PA form and possibly, as part of a song-book on the form
appropriate for books. (Form TX). (Also see Form Sr.)

(v)   *Preparing a file . In the event the rights in the song revert*
to the songwriter, the file folder should reflect that event.

(vi)   *Maintaining the files in such a way, that a person who seeks*
"something" in the file can find the "something" swiftly.

(f)   *Section 205 of the Copyright Act of 1976 concerns "recordation*
of transfers and other documents:

(a)   Conditions for Recordation. Any transfer of copyright ownership or other document pertaining to a copyright may be recorded in the Copyright Office, if the document filed for recordations bears the actual signature of the person, who executed it, or if it is accompanied by a sworn or official certification, that it is a true copy of the original, signed document.

(b)   Certificate of Recordation. The Register of Copyrights shall, upon receipt of a document, as provided by subsection (a) and of the fee provided by section 708, record the document and return it with a certification of recordation.

(c)   Recordation as Constructive Notice....

(d)   Recordation as Prerequisite to Infringement Suit.....

(e)   Priority between Conflicting Transfers.....

(f)   Priority between Conflicting Transfer of Ownership and non exclusive license...."

(g)   *Knowledge is required to register the rights obtained properly, so that the obtained rights are not lost or put in conflict or jeopardy.*

2.   *Knowledge is required to merchandise the songs.*

(a)   *Murphy's Law, "If anything can go wrong, it will," applies in the music publishing industry.*

(b)   *The proper place for a music publisher, who is submitting a lyric sheet, lead sheet, demo tape, to place his name, the name of the publishing company, the address, telephone number, telephone service, and information about the song, the songwriter, and the publisher is: EVERYWHERE.*

(c)   *Everywhere includes, but is not limited to every page of everything written, every envelope, package, label (each tape reel and cassette must have a gummed label)*

(d)   *Prepare yourself for the thought that any and every demo tape in and outside your place of business will be lost and mis-placed. Therefore, have duplicates*

(e)   *Stores have various ways of keeping track of inventory. You may wish to apply some method suitable to your operation, to keep track of:*

(i)   Paperwork
(ii)   Lead sheet originals and copies.
(iii)   Three dimensional objects, such as songbooks, sheet music, demos, masters.
(iv)   Commercially released singles, LPs tapes.
(v)   Demos "loaned" to potential users.

(f)   *You should know the track record of any hit songs in your catalog, and should have a specific page concerning each hit song in your catalog. A copy of such hit song TRACK RECORD should be given to potential users of the song.*

17.

3.   Knowledge is required to complete paperwork.

     (a)   *Knowledge is needed (and a form is needed) concerning each song, to determine whether each item of registration, contracts, merchandising tool, has been taken care of.*

     (b)   *Big and little publishers are frequently quite sloppy in their paperwork.*

     (c)   *A publisher may wonder whether or not a song has been registered with the copyright office at all, whether the registration was done originally by the songwriter or by the publisher, whether a short form COPYRIGHT ASSIGNMENT was registered.*

     (d)   *The Copyright Office is willing, for a fee, to search its files for registrations and assignments.*

     (e)   *Section 708 of the 1976 Copyright Act provides "(a) the following fees shall be paid to the Register of Copyrights: (1) for the registration of a copyright claim... $10.00.*

     "or the recordation... of a transfer of copyright ownership...

     "Six pages or less, covering no more than one title, $10.00 for each page over six and each title over one, 50 cents additional;..."

     (f)   You may be able to, <u>search</u> catalogues listing songs registered with the Copyright Office.

     (g)   Often, publishers forget whether or not some registration form or contract has been sent to the appropriate party.

     (h)   Publisher should use letters of transmittal whenever transmitting anything. "To_____. Enclosed are (name of form or contract) concerning musical composition(s) entitled... (and a filing fee of $___). Please process (or please sign and return all copies except the copy marked "your copy")" This is evidence of transmittal.

4.   Knowledge is required to license and assign rights in songs.

     (a)   The old Copyright Act of 1909, in a provision concerning "compulsory licenses," mentioned a rate to be paid by a manufacturer. (of records) to a copyright owner (the publisher) of <u>two (2¢) cents</u> for every record <u>manufactured</u>, payable <u>monthly</u>.

     (b)   The music industry, in contracts, often utilized the two (2¢) cents portion of the rate, but often reduced the records on which royalties were to be paid from records <u>manufactured</u> to records <u>sold and paid for</u>. Contracts seldom provided for monthly payments; quarterly and semi-annual payments were more commonly provided.

     (c)   Parties are free to negotiate whatever terms they may desire.

(d)   If records containing a song have already been distributed, a person, who wants to use the song on records manufactured for home use, may file a NOTICE OF INTENTION TO OBTAIN COMPULSORY LICENSE.

(e)   "With respect to each work embodied in the phonorecord, the royalty shall be either two and three-fourth cents, or one-half of one cent per minute of playing time or fraction thereof, whichever amount is larger. " The quote comes from, and further information is contained in, Section 115 of the Copyright Act of 1976.

(f)   Knowledge may come from slow and careful reading of each sentence in the small print on mechanical licenses offered by some record company.

(g)   The front of such license may show that the rate is 2.75 per song per record. The small print may say: "In the event the publisher grants a mechanical license to anyone for a lesser rate per record than the rate granted to this record company, then thereafter, automatically, the rate which this record company must pay shall be the same as the lower rate granted to the other company."

(h)   Imagine your being approached by a budget record company a record club, a record company utilizing your song solely as a mail order draw, or a premium company or a company securing the educational, military, or other market: You grant such company a low rate (especially low in the case of a premium deal). If the record company, which is discussed in the previous paragraph learns about the deal, then the record company may insist, that its rate be dropped from 2.75¢ to the lower rate, causing the publisher to lose a lot of money.

(i)   These are merely two reasons why a publisher must have ample knowledge to license and assign rights in songs.

CHAPTER 8.   ASCAP, BMI, SESAC.

ASCAP – AMERICAN SOCIETY OF COMPOSER, AUTHORS AND
PUBLISHERS.

BMI – BROADCAST MUSIC, INC.

SESAC – SESAC (That's its name) Formerly known as
THE SOCIETY OF EUROPEAN STAGE AUTHORS and
COMPOSERS.

ASCAP, BMI, and SESAC are three competing U.S. "performing"
or "performance" rights organizations, often called "performance righ
societies."

Each furnishes information about itself in booklets or pamphlets

Each receives money from radio stations and certain other users
of music.

*(SESAC is also in other licensing fields, such as phonograph
records.)*

Each keeps for itself a portion of the gross receipts, and each
pays money to publishers and to songwriters.

                    X   X   X

A copyright is a bundle of rights.

One of the rights in a copyright is the right to play the
musical composition on radio. *"Small performance rights"* include
the radio playing right and some other rights.

The performance rights society has contracts with songwriters an
publishers.

The performance rights society <u>receives rights</u> *(the right to
play the song on radio and other small performance rights) and
<u>promises to pay</u> money to the songwriters and publishers.*

A radio station <u>may not</u> play records containing music protected
by copyright <u>unless</u> the radio station is receiving the right to play
the music.

A radio station <u>may</u> play records containing music protected by
copyright, <u>if</u> the radio station is exempt or <u>if</u> it receives the right
to play the music.

A publisher would have to send out thousand of licenses per
song,if a publisher licensed each radio station directly himself or
herself.

Both parties, the copyright owners, (the songwriter and for the
publisher) and the copyright user (the radio station, the television
station, the user of background music, etc.) avoid the problem of
licensing each song to each station by utilizing a performance rights
organization *(ASCAP, BMI, SESAC)*.

Thousands of songwriters and publishers belong to ASCAP; their radio play and other small performance rights flow to ASCAP.

ASCAP provides forms for the use of ASCAP songwriters and publishers to notify ASCAP about each new song.

ASCAP licenses each radio station in a license-contract to use every song in ASCAP catalog.

The radio station pays a fee to *ASCAP*. The fee is not a <u>per song</u> fee. The fee is for the use of the *ASCAP* catalog (for all the songs in the *ASCAP* catalog).

ASCAP collects information concerning airplay (which song was played how many times on which station and other information), considers how much money is available for distribution to songwriters and publishers, and distributes the money.

BMI competes with ASCAP to obtain new songwriter and publisher members and to obtain new songs.

A songwriter may belong only to one performance rights society <u>at a time</u>.

A publisher may sign one contract with ASCAP(using one fictitious firm name such as <u>Suite</u> Seven Music) and a second contract with BMI (using another fictitious firm name such as <u>Room</u> Seven Music)

A publisher places songs written by ASCAP songwriters in the publisher's *ASCAP* firm, and songs written by BMI songwriters in the publisher's *BMI* firm, and songs written by *SESAC* songwriters in the publisher's *SESAC* firm.

BMI has its system of gathering information to calculate payments to songwriters and publishers.

CHAPTER 9. JOINING ASCAP, BMI, SESAC.

A person, who becomes a publisher, will want to receive money from a performance rights organization.

A publisher may go to the performance rights organization he selects, and may say, "I want to join."

The organization may say, "*You can join <u>after</u> you have a song on a record (or in a motion picture or television production).*"

A publisher may say "I have a list of names, which I **may** call my publishing company, the names are set forth in the order of preferen Please clear a name, that I may use."

The performing rights organization will match the names on the publisher's list against lists of names of publishers which already belong to the performing rights organizations. (This matching <u>may</u> take weeks.)

The performing rights organization may say, "*Your first three choices were not available. Your fourth choice is available. We will hold it for you for three months.*"

The publisher may ask for extensions of time to reserve the name longer.

Eventually, the publisher informs a record company, which utilizes one of the publisher's songs,   "*The song will be placed in ASCAP. My ASCAP publishing company is* _____.*"*

The record company places the information on a record label.

When the record has been pressed or released, the publisher is eligible for membership in the performance rights organization.

The publisher notifies the performance rights organization, that he is now eligible to join.

The performance rights organization sends a contract to the publisher. The contract has space for the publisher to list songs.

The publisher should check with each performance rights organization, concerning their policy regarding (1) initial one-time application or membership fee, and (2) annual fees.

CHAPTER 10.   FICTITIOUS NAME CERTIFICATE.

Most music publishers have the word "music" and/or "publisher" in their name. For example: Room Seven Music. or Room Seven Publishing Co. or Room Seven Music Publishers.

California requires, that persons (the term "persons" includes individuals, partners, corporations) doing business under a fictitious name (Room Seven Music is a fictitious name.) file a certificate on doing business under a fictitious name with the County Clerk *and advertise* the contents of the certificate in an appropriate newspaper.

A newspaper can petition to the Superior Court for an order recognizing such newspaper as one with "general circulation" and therefore authorized to carry "legal advertising" (advertising required by law.)

Special newspapers servicing attorneys (*such as the Metropolitan News and the Daily Journal in Los Angeles)* and recognized neighborhood newspapers obtain income from carrying such "legal advertising" (such as the certificate of doing business under a fictitious name).

The new publisher has another problem of the *"Which came first, the chicken or the egg?"* variety.

Should the publisher file the certificate and advertise the contents, when the publisher first starts his business?

If he does, what happens if the performance rights organization refuses to clear that name and insists that the publisher use another name? As a practical matter, the publisher will probably discontinue using the uncleared name and will start using a cleared name.

To avoid the problems connected with changing a name, a new publisher may want to: *FIRST* - clear the name with the performance rights organization he wants to join (*ASCAP, BMI, SESAC)* SECOND - *File the fictitious name certificate.*

Before a publisher can open a bank account in a fictitious name, the bank may require a copy of the filed and advertised certificate of doing business under a fictitious name.

A new publisher may want to open a bank account on the day he starts in business, and may not want to wait until after the performance rights society has cleared the name and the fictitious name certificate has been filed.

The publisher may open the bank account in his own name.

His name and address can be printed on checks. If the publisher wants to do so, and the bank agrees, the fictitious name can be printed as part of the address.

Real Name: William Storm Hale

Address: Suite Seven Music

_____ Boulevard

City, State, Zip

(CERTIFICATE OF FICTITIOUS NAME)

(Followed by instructions)

CHAPTER 11. U.S. EMPLOYER IDENTIFICATION NUMBER.

Individuals have social security numbers.

Businesses have U.S. Employer Identification Numbers.

Individuals, who are in business, should apply for U.S. Employer Identification Numbers.

Individuals, who are in business, should apply for U.S. Employer Identification Numbers, whether or not the individual plans to have employees.

An individual, who is in business as a music publisher may have a profitable year or an unprofitable year.

The individual should report his income and expenses on Schedule C of Form 1040.

Schedule C has a space for the Employer Identification Number.

The presence of a number in the space supports the concept that the individual is a music publisher for business purposes (rather than hobby purposes).

A person (*individual, partnership, corporation),* which requests a U.S. Employer Identification number will receive employer tax Forms 941 and 940 from the United States.

These forms concern wages paid to employees: gross wages, amounts withheld for income tax, Social Security taxes (both the amount withheld and the employer's additional portion).

If there are no employees and no salaries, merely fill in the spaces on the tax form with "O" or "NONE."

The form to apply for a U.S. Employer Identification Number is free and is available at offices of the Internal Revenue Service. *(look under "United States" in the white pages telephone Directory).*

Be sure to keep a copy of the information, that you provide in your application for a U.S. Employer Identification Number and every other form. The Form is SS-4.

The completed application form is sent to the appropriate local office of the District Director of the Internal Revenue Service.

See the reverse side of the form for instructions, concerning completing the form and where to send it.

The IRS will send you the number, usually within ten days. PLEASE DON'T LOSE THE NUMBER. Write it in this book, the cover of your check book, your Rollodex, and prepare a file:

TAX: US: EMPLOYER IDENTIFICATION NO. _____

CHAPTER 12.   EMPLOYEES

The cost of each employee may be 120% to 200% of the gross salary.

If an employee tells you, that he is worth more than you are paying him, consider whether he is worth more than his cost to you.

The cost of an employee includes:

1. *Gross salary*
2. *Employer taxes to the U.S.*
3. *Employer taxes to the state*
4. *Workers Compensation.*

The cost to you also includes:

5. *The cost of your time teaching an employee.*
6. *The cost of your time trying to find your employee's errors and finding them, trying to make up those errors.*
7. *The cost of your time preparing a payroll, the payroll journal, the payroll ledger, balancing the payroll checkbook, preparing Federal and State quarterly and annual tax returns.*
8. *The cost of your time listening to your employee's personal life headaches, worries, dreams, ambitions, bellyaches et al.*
9. *The cost of your time worrying about all your employees.*

The gap between the cost of an employee to an employer is widened even further by the amount of payroll deductions taken from an employees salary.

Gross salary

-   U.S. Income tax withheld
-   State Income tax withheld
-   U.S. Social Security withheld
-   State disability insurance or unemployment insurance withheld.
=   Net take-home salary.

Many new publishers dread the thought of having employees.

Sometimes, the employee problem is solved simply; the publisher decides to have no employees.

The publisher decides to do everything himself or through independent contractors.

Or a publisher may invest in employees, hoping that the cost in gross salary, extra direct costs, costs of rent, telephone, furniture, overhead, etc. will be worthwhile.

CHAPTER 13.   PAYROLL PROBLEMS + PROCEDURES

The publisher must take into consideration the following payroll problems:

1.   *Each payroll check Complete gross, amounts withheld, net. Use a separate checking account for payroll.*

2.   *Enter information in a payroll journal and a separate payroll ledger for each employee. Inquire about a "one-write" system, in which the check stub, payroll journal, payroll ledger are filled out simultaneously.*

3.   *Make all deposits on account* promptly. *Depending on the size of your payroll, deposits may have to be made within three days after your payroll, or monthly, or quarterly. (if you have a union recording session payroll which is large enough to require deposits on account within three days, be sure to make the deposit promptly. Deposits, to the Internal Revenue Service, as payments on account, are made to a bank; deposits are accompanied by an IBM type card furnished by the employer.*

4.   *Employer tax payments and payments for workers compensation should be made from the payroll book, for the reason, that they are found most easily in* **that** *book. (on the otherhand, estimated* income *taxes, which the individual pays for himself, should be made out of the general business account.)*

5.   *It is absolutely essential that no check from the payroll account ever bounce. Some publishers maintain a base amount which exceeds a week's gross salary in the account, and on the day that the payroll is calculated, transfer 115% of the gross payroll to the payroll account from the general business account.*

6.   *The extra 15% may be enough to cover (i) employer's share of social security taxes, (ii) employer's unemployment taxes payable to the State, (iii) U.S. FUTA (Federal Unemployment Tax Act) (iv) Worker's Compensation rates on an office worker's salary.*

7.   *Extra amounts must be added to the payroll account, in the event the publisher has an union recording session, to cover extra payments to trust funds and additional Worker's Compensation.*

8.   *The payroll preparer needs to look at separate tables to compute:*

    a)   U.S. income tax to be withheld.
    b)   State income tax to be withheld.
    c)   Social Security to be withheld.
    d)   Disability insurance to be withheld.

9.   *The amount of income tax withheld on the salary is not the same for all employees. Factors include:*

    a)   Whether the employee is married or single.
    b)   The number of exemptions <u>claimed</u> (which is different from the number of exemptions claimed on the annual income tax returns).
    c)   Whether any rule <u>waiving</u> withholding any taxes is applicable.

10.   Try to calculate and pay all taxes payable for the quarter ending in December before the year is over. Try to complete preparat on all W-2 forms before the year is over. That way, employer taxes and expenses pertinent to a taxable calendar year will be paid during the calendar year.

11.   It is quite likely, that you are less than 100% perfect in computing all your payroll, payroll deductions, net wages, payroll deposits during the year. Part of your routine cost of doing business is finding errors, and correcting them.

12.   You may find, that the days just before and after Christmas are good days to clean up payroll records and to prepare W-2s.

13.   Employers are required to send W-2s to employees no later than January 31.

CHAPTER 14. THE SONGWRITER - NEEDED INFORMATION.

The publisher may find it _simple_ to fill in the blanks of a songwriter-publisher _contract_.

1. Date
2. Publisher's name.
3. Songwriter's name.
4. Song.

The publisher may find it _simple_ to prepare a _Copyright Office Form PA_.

1. Song
2. Songwriter's name.
3. Songwriter's year of birth.
4. Songwriter's pseudonym (if any).
5. Contribution, lyrics, music, arrangement, etc.
6. Songwriter's residence or citizenship.
7. etc.

The publisher may find it simple to prepare a _BMI song clearance form_:

1. Song
2. Songwriter's name
3. Songwriter's Address
4. Songwriter's Social Security number
5. Songwriter's Share of song
6. Songwriter's Performance rights society

The publisher may find it easy to prepare _royalty statements_

1. Song
2. Amount received by the publisher
3. Publisher's share
4. Songwriters share for all writers.
5. Agreed upon percentage for the individual writers if there are more than one writer.

The publisher may find it simple to prepare a U.S. Internal Revenue Service _Form 1099_

1. Songwriter's name
2. Songwriter's address
3. Songwriter's Social Security number
4. Songwriter's total royalty for the year.

The publisher may face a lot of problems, if he does not promptly complete a SONGWRITER'S INFORMATION SHEET at the time he first deals with the songwriter.

CHAPTER 15.   SONGWRITER'S INFORMATION SHEET

NAME _____
     Last   Name,   First Name   Middle   Name

PSEUDONYM _____
As Songwriter   Last Name   First   Name   Middle Name

DRIVER'S LICENSE DESCRIPTION: _____ _____

____ _____ _____ _____ _____ _____
Sex   Hair   Eyes   Height   Weight   Date of Birth

OTHER IDENTIFICATION: _____ _____
                  Social Security No.   Credit Card + Number

_____ _____
Auto Club + Number   Union + Number

MAIL ADDRESS: c/o _____

_____
No. Street   Apartment   City   State   Zip

If mail is returned, please send mail to me c/o _____

_____
No.   Street   Apartment City   State   Zip

To reach me by phone, try these numbers:

        Business telephone
        Home telephone
        Answering Service
        Parent(s) telephone
        Other telephones
        Other telephones
        Other telephones

This space is left for future address.

Please mark through obsolete addresses and telephones.

CHAPTER 16.   SONGWRITER'S LIST OF SONGS.

SONGWRITER: _____
                Last   Name   First Name   Middle   Name

S% = Songwriter's Percentage
P% = Publisher's Percentage

Date of Contract	Song	Music by	S%	Lyrics by	S%	Administrative Publisher	P%	CO-publisher	P%

CHAPTER 17. SONGWRITER'S ROYALTY SUMMARY

(PUBLISHER'S <u>SONGWRITER'S LEDGER</u>)

Date, Check No.	Explanation	Debit	Credit	Balance
	Examples:			
3/1	Publisher received CBS royalties and computed S royalties as:	-	500	500
3/15	Publisher received RCA royalties, and computes S royalties as:	-	300	800
3/28	Publisher received Capitol royalties and computed S royalties as:	-	400	1200
6/30	Memo: Royalties payable for the period ending 6/30 is $1200			
8/1	Publisher received royalties from CBS, and computed S royalties as	-	500	1700
9/1 #1001	Publisher paid royalties to S for the period ending 6/30	1200	-	500
11/15 #1002	Publisher paid advance royalties	1000	-	Overpaid (500)
12/31	Memo - Publisher royalties have been over-paid for period ending 12/31			

CHAPTER 18.   DON'T OVERPAY YOUR SONGWRITER
(THE PUBLISHER AS A PIGEON)

Supposedly the songwriter is a manufacturer, who is talented in creation of songs.

THe songwriter may or may not know a lot about business.

Possibly, the songwriter thinks, or wants to think, that his publisher is cheating him or her.

This thinking, or pretend-thinking, allows the songwriter to justify his, ruthlessly, taking advantage of the publisher.

The songwriter may seek advances from the publisher.

The advance may be an advance against royalties for a specific song only, or an advance against any royalties for any and all songs.

The advance may be a regular amount paid regularly (weekly, monthly, etc.)

Or, the advance may be a *"need advance."* The songwriter says *"I need money for rent."(I spent all mine on clothing). "I need money to repair my car." (I spent the entire advance on a down-payment for a car I can't afford.) "I need money for food." (I spent the food budget on booze and drugs).*

The plucking may be *$5 for gas, $20 for a shot, $500 for an abortion* (You name it.)

The publisher may play this game of giving advances, for the same reason any distributor may give advances to a manufacturer: he thinks that it is a good business practice.

If the publisher uses checks to pay advances, the publisher should clearly show on the check the payee *("Sam Songwriter")* and the reason for the check *("Advance against all royalties").*

The pattern of the entreating songwriter, includes attempting to foul up the publisher's record keeping, so that the publisher will forget to recoup the advance.

To that end, the songwriter may say, *"I can't use the check. I don't have time to cash it. I don't have identification to cash it. My creditor won't accept a third party check. Please give me cash."*

The publisher <u>should</u> write a check to the songwriter, if at all possible. The songwriter <u>should</u> endorse on the back of the check, *"I acknowledge receipt of $_____ in cash from Publisher"* and should sign his name.

The publisher should be sure to place that check with the other returned from the bank.

The checkstub should clearly state *"MEMO-PUBLISHER CASHED THIS CHECK FOR SONGWRITER."* Thus the person, who reconciles the bank account will be made aware.

The person, who prepares the journal listing checks, should list the check in regular order, and should write *"MEMO-PUBLISHER CASHED THIS CHECK FOR SONGWRITER."*

The person, who prepares the *SONGWRITER'S ROYALTY SUMMARY (Publisher's Songwriters Ledger)* should also indicate the check date and number, and the *"MEMO - PUBLISHER CASHED THIS CHECK FOR SONGWRITER*

The publisher may be plucked by the songwriter at a time the publisher does not have a checkbook available.

In such a case, the publisher should dictate to the songwriter, and the songwriter should write in his/her own hand so that the songwriter will find it difficult to deny receiving the advance: I acknowledge receipt of _____ dollars, ($_____)

from_____, music publisher, on_____ as an advance against any and all royalties."

_____

Name:

Social Security No:

If the songwriter refuses to prepare a receipt, the songwriter shows, that the songwriter is not hungry enough to need the advance.

The publisher should use a check as a memorandum, showing on the check stub the normal payee (*"Sam Seanwriter"*), the reason (*"Advance against all royalties"*) the fact that it is a MEMO, and that the check was not cashed.

The cost of bookkeeping is high, even when everything is orderly; the cost of bookkeeping and calculation of advances against royalties is even more expensive, when the royalty preparer finds that record keeping concerning advances was not orderly.

CHAPTER 19. THE PUBLISHER IS IN THE MONEY BUSINESS

A publisher may pay some expenses in advance (*rent for the month is payable in advance*), some expenses when incurred (cash for a parking meter, some expenses after they are incurred (a meal paid for with a credit card.)

All these expenses are paid for within weeks of the day they were incurred.

Some items, such as cars and houses and other *"big ticket"* items are paid for on the installment plan. Usually, when the publisher pays installments, a portion of each payment is for interest.

Interest is money paid for the use of money.

The publisher receives royalties, calculates the portion of receipts payable to the songwriter and the portion, which he may use for other business expenses and for profit.

For example:

Receipt - The publisher receives $10,000 from MCA
Calculation - The publisher retains $5,000 and credits
$5,000 to the songwriter's account.
(the publisher owes $5,000 to the songwriter)

The money may be paid by the record company to the publisher on a semi-annual basis, ninety days after the end of the semi-annual period.

For example:

Royalty Period: January-June, Year 1
Payment to Publisher: September 28, Year 1
Amount received by Publisher: $10,000.

The publisher may pay the songwriter on a semi-annual basis, ninety days after the end of the semi-annual period.

For example:

Royalty Period: July-December, Year 1
Payment to Songwriter: March 31, Year 2
Amount paid by publisher: $5,000

The publisher has use of the $5,000, eventually paid to the songwriter, from the day it is received by the publisher to the day it is paid out by the publisher.

Received By Publisher: September 28, Year 1
Paid By Publisher: March 31, Year 2
Use of Money: 6 months.

The publisher can invest the $5,000 invested at simple interest of 10% per annum for 6 months equals $250.

$250 extra income may not appear to be much compared to the publisher's gross receipts of $10,000.

But a publisher incurs expenses. The $10,000 gross receipts, less songwriters royalties equals $5,000. The $5,000, less expenses for rent, employees, independent contractors, travel, business entertainment, etc. may shrink to $500 net profit from business operations.

Now Compare:

Profit from business operations: $500
*Extra Income from interest earned with
the songwriter's royalties held for half
a year* $250

TOTAL PROFIT $750

Interest income is 1/3 of the total profit. $250 is 1/3 of $750.

Now you can readily see why it may be important for publishers to pay songwriters according to contract, and not any faster.

CHAPTER 20. UNCLE SAM IS IN THE TAXING BUSINESS

Most taxpayers use the calendar year as their tax year. Some taxpayers utilize a fiscal year (a year ending on a date other than December 31) as their tax year. In this chapter, we are going to assume that the tax year is the same as the calendar year.

A taxpayer may use the <u>cash basis</u> of accounting. *(all income is reported in the year of receipt, all expenses are reported in the year they are paid.)*

A taxpayer may use the <u>accrual method</u> of accounting. *(All income is reported when the right to it is created; all expenses are reported when the obligation to pay them are incurred.)*

There are variations, so that taxpayers generally on the cash basis don't always use it, and taxpayers generally on the accrual don't always use it.

In the previous chapter, the publisher received royalties in Year 1. and paid the songwriter in Year 2.

A taxpayer, who reports income and expenses on the calendar year basis, may report for Year 1.

GROSS INCOME		$10,000
Less Expenses		
Songwriters Royalties	$ 0	
Other Expenses	4,500	
Total Expenses	4,500	4,500
NET PROFIT		5,500

If the taxpayer pays taxes on the $5,500 net profit at the rate of 30%, then the taxes will be $1650.

PRE-TAX NET PROFIT	5,500
Less Income Taxes	1,650
Profit left after taxes	3,850

But the Taxpayer faces the obligation of paying the songwriter $5,000 on March 31, Year 2, and he wants to report the $5000 songwriter royalties as an expense in Year 1.

Gross Income		10,000
Less Expenses		
Songwriters Royalties	$5,000	
Other expenses	4,500	
Total Expenses	9,500	9,500
NET PROFIT		500

If, for purposes of simple comparisons, the taxpayer pays taxes on the $500 net profit at the rate of 30%, then the taxes will be $150.

```
PRE-TAX NET PROFIT                    $500
     Less Income Taxes                 150
     Profit Left After Taxes          $350
```

Question: How can the publisher deduct the $5000 as an expense in year 1, although the publisher does not pay the money to the songwriter in Year 1?

Answer: With difficulty.

The publisher may set up a double entry bookkeeping entry on the last day of the year.

```
Royalty Expense                    $5,000

     Royalties Payable                          $5,000
```
(to record royalties payable next year, based on royalty income received this year by publisher.)

The Royalty Expense shows up on the BALANCE SHEET dated December 31, Year 1.

That system, of deducting a royalty expense in Year 1, might be challenged by the Internal Revenue Service.

The Internal Revenue Service may argue that , if taxpayer is on the <u>cash basis</u>, then taxpayer may not deduct anything until taxpayer spends the cash (that is, pays the $5000 in Year 2).

The Internal Revenue Service may argue that, if taxpayer is on the <u>accrual basis</u>, then the $5000 should be deducted when the obligation is incurred, and that according to the contract between the songwriter and the publisher, there is no obligation to pay royalties based on the publisher's income during July-December Year 1, until March 30, Year 2.

To avoid arguments, a publisher may provide in the songwriter-publisher contract, that the royalty periods run December-May and June-November, that royalties are payable to the songwriter no later than 90 days after the end of each royalty period; <u>and</u> the publisher will pay royalties for the June-November period before December 31.

There are other variations, which may be explored by the publisher and his tax consultant.

CHAPTER 21.   THE SONG PINK LABEL FILE FOLDER

A file folder containing important papers containing a song, should have a special color label which is used by the publisher only for *SONG* files.

Pink is a fine color for the label.

The first word on the label should be song.   In the event the file folder is ever misplaced, *(For example, if instead of being filed in the file cabinet reserved for the song files, the folder is filed in general active or inactive files),* then the file folder may be searched for in alphabetical order under *SONG*.

The word SONG should be followed by the song's title.

For Example: *SONG: MR INFORMATION.*

The third item to be placed on the top line of the Pink label is the year in which the first of the following occurs:

1. *The songwriter - publisher contract*
2. *The song is published*
3. *The song is registered with the Copyright Office.*

On the second line of the label, list the songwriters.   If any songwriter died, indicate DIED and the year, and who has been granted the performance rights.

On the third line of the label, list the specific publishing firm, in which the song was placed and list the performance rights organization with which the song is connected.   In the event, the song has more than one publisher or one writer or one performance rights organization, you should show that.

You need not use the whole name of the publishing company. *(for example, you need not write "Room Seven Music, BMI.")* you may shorten this to "Room 7, B".

A for   *ASCAP*
B for   *BMI*
S for   *SESAC*

The file folder of a song should contain a photocopy or carbon of each Copyright Office *application assignment or other recorded matter, (for Example:Form E and Form U for pre-1978 song and notice of use registrations, Form R for pre-1978 renewal registrations, Form PA and Form RE for post-1977 song and renewal registrations.)*

The file folder should contain a copy of the performance rights, society registration.   In the event, the publisher has filed, not only his own song clearance form, but also forms for co-publishers and songwriter(s), a copy of each such additional registration should be in the song file folder.

It is important, that the form (the Copyright Office Form, the performance rights society form) indicates whether it is a copy of:

1.   A form the publisher never sent anywhere.

2.   A form, which bounced because it was completed improperly.

3.   A form, which was accepted; such a form should show
some indication of acceptance *(such as a "received _____"
date rubber stamp, a Copyright Office Registration Number, or
whatever is applicable to the specific form.)*

The *SONG* file folder should contain a lyric sheet and a lead
sheet.

The song file folder should contain a document entitled:
SOUND RECORDINGS AND PRINTED MATTER.

On this document, the publisher should make entries concerning
demos, masters, records, LPs, tapes, sheet music, music books, etc.

The song file should contain a *SONG PAPERWORK CHECKLIST*
which will list the items mentioned in this chapter, and indicate which
items are in the file (and by absence of a checkmark, the list will
show which items are not in the file).

The *SONG* file may contain, if the publisher wishes, cassettes,
demo discs and records Since these are relatively thin and small,
their presence may not make the *SONG* file too bulky. Also, since they
are small, they may be lost elsewhere.

CHAPTER 22. THE LEAD SHEET FILE FOLDER.

Some lead sheets are prepared on 8½" X 11" paper or 8½" X 13"; either a regular letter sized folder or legal size paper folder can be used. Onion skin or regular bond may be used.

Copies are made on the same type of paper or on a different type. (Same type: Bond original, bond copy. Different type: Onion skin original, ozalid copy.)

The lead sheets can be trimmed down, at the corners on both sides, bottom or on the top, as needed by the publisher.

Each file folder should be clearly marked with a label *(preferably pink the same color as the song file folder)*. It would be convenient to keep the two sets of files as close together as possible.

The words *LEAD SHEET*_____ *Name of song,* _____*year,* should appear on the top line of the label.

The file may also contain samples of printed sheet music, arrangements of the song, and other written versions of the song.

The *year*_____ should be the first year, in which anything in the file was created.

In the event any file becomes too fat for comfort another file should be created as the need arises.

The publisher may place earlier Lead Sheets and sheet music in one file.

The second file created should begin from the year listed on the first item inserted in the folder.

Ample space should be allowed for oversize file folders.

Each song, for which the publisher has a Lead Sheet should be in alphabetical order.

It is important to keep everything that pertains to your business at present, tomorrow or in the future at hand and easily accessible; lost documentation can lose you money and cause you anguish, distrust from your clients and loss of faith, as well as further unnecessary paperwork to try and make up the loss, and embarrassment.

CHAPTER 23. ANSCR - THE ALPHA-NUMERIC SYSTEM FOR CLASSIFICATION OF RECORDINGS.

"*ANSCR*," pronounced "answer", by Caroline Saheb-Ettaba and Roger B. McFarland, published by Bro-Dart Publishing Company, Williamsport, Pennsylvania, 1969, is a book, which deals with classification of sound recordings of all types, whether on plastic disc or on tape (*reel to reel, cartridge, cassette*) or in any other physical format. It is a classification system devised specifically for sound recordings and is called the Alpha-Numeric System for Classification of Recordings.

The *ANSCR CLASSIFICATION SCHEME* includes letters of the alphabet.

> *A - Music Appreciation - History and Commentary*
> *G - Solar Instrumental Music*
> *H - Band Music*
> *M - Popular Music*
> > *MA Pop Music*
> > *MC Country and Western Music*
> > *MJ Jazz.*

etc.

Each *CATEGORY* is broken down further. The following concerns *CATEGORY MJ-Jazz Music.*

MJ 1. Types of Recordings to be classed in Category MJ

"Greatest Hits," (Louis Armstrong) Columbia CS 9438
"Blue Bechet"   (Sidney Becket)   RCA Victor LPV 535
"Ugetsa"   (Art Blakey)   Riverside   53022

MJ 2. FORMATION OF CLASS NUMBER IN CATEGORY MJ

A. Term One

Term One is composed of the letters "MJ"

B. Term Two

Three types of entry may be used.

1. PERFORMER ENTRY   .
Use the surname of the featured performer or the name of the performin
group to form term two when classifying recordings which feature one
performer or one performing.

"*Day in the Life*"	MJ
Wes Montgomery	.MONT
A & M SP 3001	DL
	M 01

"*Shades of Blue*"	MJ
Billie Holiday	.HOLI
Sunset 5147	SB
	H 47

2. COMPOSER ENTRY

' ' '

3. COLLECTIONS ENTRY

' ' '

C. Term Three

Always use the ablum title to form Term Three....

D. Term Four

The same name used for the PERFORMER ENTRY in Term Two is used to form the alpha symbol in Term Four...

X   X   X

The book ANSCR, is over 200 pages long. The above information is merely designed to illustrate that attention has been paid to the difficult problem of filing and finding records and tapes. The publisher, BRO-DART Publishing Company, WILLIAMSPORT, PENNSYLVANIA, is a leader in servicing libraries.

The price of the book was $10. and still may be.

CHAPTER 24. WHICH SONG IS ON WHICH RECORD?

ASCAP furnishes a form known as:

ASCAP Record Information Sheet, to writers who want to join ASCAP.

The form has columns for:

1. *Title of composition*
2. *Recording Artist.*
3. *Record Co.*
4. *Indicate Record No: and "S" for Singles,"LP" for Albums*
5. *Writers (full names)*
6. *Publisher.*

We found a good use for the form. We crossed out the word ASCAP, *if not all songs in an LP were totally ASCAP songs. If all songs were totally BMI songs, we wrote BMI above the crossed out* ASCAP

Then we wrote SIDE 1 in the first line listing song titles.

Thereunder we wrote the names of the respective titles, and SIDE 1 and filled in the other columns.

We often use ditto (") marks for purposes of speed and legibility.

To avoid confusion caused by the length of some titles of songs or other information requiring more than one line, we numbered the songs on Side 1.

Then we skipped a line, wrote SIDE 2 in the next line.

We continued the numerical sequence. Thus, if SIDE 1 had five songs, the first song on SIDE 2 would be "#6."

In the upper left hand column of the form, to the left of the title of the form, we experimentally wrote:

(Full name of the album)   (ANSCR Symbols).
(Artist)
(Record Co. and Number)

When this form was completed, it was photocopied numerous times.

(1) *THE ORIGINAL was filed in alphabetical order, by* <u>Full name of</u> <u>the album</u> *in a file folder using a GREEN LABEL entitled:*

SONG INDEX: Full name of the Album.   Year_____

(2)   One copy was filed in a *GREEN LABEL* file folder entitled:

SONG INDEX: Full name of the artist Years_____.   (*Note:*

For each artist, the albums are placed in alphabetical order by title).

(3)   One copy was filed in <u>each</u> *SONG file (pink color label)* in which the publisher had an interest (as songwriter or publisher)

(4)   In the event the publisher has an economic interest in the record as ARTIST or as PRODUCER, then a copy may be placed into respective *GREEN LABEL* files:

    SONG INDEX.   *Artist's Royalty Interest* _____Years
    SONG INDEX.   *Manager's Royalty Interest* _____Years
    SONG INDEX.   *Producer's Royalty Interest*_____Years

    SONG INDEX.   *Some other Royalty Interest*_____Years

(5)   One copy was filed in each SONGWRITER file, if the publisher owed the duty to pay royalties to the songwriter. If the publisher did not owe the duty to pay royalties to the songwriter, because a co-publisher or administrative publisher had that duty, a copy of the form would be filed in the SONGWRITER file <u>with</u> the notation on the form concerning the royalty arrangement.

(6)   One copy was filed in each PUBLISHER file for any other PUBLISHER concerned with the song (administrative publisher, co-publisher, foreign publisher).

CHAPTER 25. COSTS OF COPIES AND FILES.

Your initial reaction to the number of copies and files may be: *Are all these copies and files necessary?* The simple answer is "No."

Then why go to so much trouble, even for songs on albums which did not sell well?

The answer concerns the publisher's risky show business bet. The publisher bets time and money, in order to win.

Winning includes:

1. *Being able to find a lead sheet, lyric sheet, demo, or record of a song, when it is wanted.*

2. *Being able to find the sought item* _swiftly_. *It is very depressing for a publisher, who has orally prepared an artist to consider a song, to be unable to* _swiftly_ *find the appropriate lyric sheet, lead sheet, demo or record.*

3. *Keeping track of royalties which may be due. Even the biggest record companies have been sued for royalties. Often, a courteous letter to the record company inquiring about royalties may cause record companies to pay royalties. Sometimes mail may not be delivered to a publisher who has moved, and the record company may receive the undelivered envelope; the record company may then wait until the publisher contacts the record company, before trying to again mail royalties to the publisher.*

4. *Maintaining a full* _library of records_ *containing the songs. Sometimes records disappear and have to be found at great expense.*

5. *Being able to find which songwriters and co-publishers should be* _paid_ *which share of royalty income received by the publisher from various sources.*

6. *Having files in good order so that persons interested in buying the publishing company will pay the maximum price (without deducting, in their own minds, the tremendous cost of cleaning up the files)*

7. *Creating files at minimum expense, paying wages and fees to persons familiar with the facts at the time each LP is available, rather than having to pay for time spent trying to re-construct files and finding missing portions.*

You may be making thousands of copies, using thousands of regular letter and legal size file folders, and many extra-large file folders for lead sheets.

Thus it behooves you to spend time comparing prices quoted by both _retail_ and _wholesale_ office supply and paper companies, as well as costs of photocopies and photocopiers.

CHAPTER 26. INCOME FROM HITS AND NON HITS.

As a very practical matter, record companies pay more money in mechanical license fees for songs which are <u>not</u> hits than for songs which are hits!!!

Consider the arithmetic which supports this outrageous statement.

If a single is not a hit, and most are not hits, then all of the mechanicals are paid for <u>non-hits</u>.

If is a hit, usually only one song is a hit, while the song on the reverse side is a non-hit hitching a lucky ride. Thus an equal amount of mechanicals is paid for the hit and the non-hit.

Most LPs contain fewer hits than non-hits. Even many so-called "HITS OF _____" LPs merely contain a re-packaged mixture
                    (artist)
of hits and non-hits.

Thus, one of the tasks of a publisher is to have his songs, whether hit or non-hit, placed on LPs.

The decision of which song is accepted for an LP involves many factors. One factor may be how well the song fits into the LP. Another factor may be how much, in money, the decision maker may receive if the song is included in the LP. A third factor concerns the principles of "one hand washes the other" and of "friendship." Thus a publisher may be able to place a non-hit song in a record album.

Songwriters often copy their own songs, especially, when the original song and the copy are owned by the same publisher. Thus, a library of lyric sheets, lead sheets, demos, and records can be used by a songwriter, who is asked to write songs swiftly for a specific record or movie project.

CHAPTER 27. COPYRIGHT OFFICE FORMS.

The publisher should be aware of the variety of pre-1978 and post-1977 forms.

Pre-1978 forms included, but were not limited to:

Form A - For books, including songbooks some publishers prepared books consisting of a title page such as "SONG BOOK No. 1," placed a copyright notice on the title page, prepared a TABLE OF CONTENTS, added numerous copies of lyric sheets and lead sheets, offered the book for sale to the public, filed Form A with the Copyright Office and simultaneously submitted two copies of the song book and the filing fee of $6.00.

Form E - For both unpublished and published musical compositions. Publishers might seek an E (E for Musical composition; EU for unpublished) registration by sending Form E, an unpublished copy of a lead sheet, and $6,00. Some publishers offered or distributed copies of the lead sheet to the general public and sought an E P (E for musical composition, P for published) registration, two (2) copies of the lead sheet, and $6.00.

FORM U - Notice of use. This form was filed to give notice that the song had been recorded, and therefore was available for recording by anyone else who wanted to record the song after furnishing appropriate notice of intention to record. Before 1978, if a publisher failed to file Form U when due, as long as it was unfiled, a "pirate" could use the song on his records without having to pay any mechanical licenses.

Form U is no longer used under the new copyright act.

FORM R- Renewal. This form was used in the 28th year after initial registration or publication of a work, to file a claim for copyright for a second 28 year period of copyright protection. Congress, commencing in 1962, added extension periods to the duration of the second 28 year period.

The pre-1978 forms were replaced in 1978 with other forms, which include, but are not limited to:

Form TX - Books. See the discussion under Form A. Also see the instructions on the pages which come with the form. You may wish to register the songbook as an unpublished manuscript (if it is unpublished or as a published book (if it is published). Under the old 1909 Copyright Act (which was effective until December 31, 1977), unpublished book-type manuscripts could not be registered on Form A. (Sometimes the Copyright Office accepted unpublished works containing many songs with Form D or Form E).

Form PA -Performing Arts. This form takes the place of old Form E for unpublished and for published musical compositions.

Form RE - *This form replaces old Form R.* _Please_ *read the*
Copyright Office Circular and the instructions accompanying
Form RE for details of when and how to use Form E.

One of the reasons for coding SONG files by year is to
assist the publisher to file Form RE at the appropriate
time.

The Copyright Office will search its files and report to
inquirers the results of the search. The fee is $10.00 per hour.

Also, a person may search published volumes of Copyright Office
Catalogs.

You may wish to send for the Copyright Office Circular which
discusses how to make searches concerning copyrights.

The duration of copyright protection varies for works depending
on the circumstances. A Copyright Office circular discusses duration.

Form SR - *This form replaces old Form N.*

When To Use Form SR: *Form SR is the appropriate*
application to use for copyright registration covering a sound
recording. It should be used where the copyright claim is
limited to the sound recording itself, and it should also be used
where the same copyright claimant is seeking to register not only
the sound recording but also the musical, dramatic or literary work
embodied in the sound recording. Both published and unpublished
works can be registered on Form SR .

CHAPTER 28. REQUEST LETTER TO COPYRIGHT OFFICE

Register of Copyrights
Library of Congress
Washington D.C. 20559

Dear Gentlepersons:

Please send me:

1.   One copy of every circular.
2.   Fifty (50) copies of Form PA and of Form SR.
3.   Ten (10) copies of every other form.

Please put me on your mailing list.

Sincerely,

CHAPTER 29. SEARCH LETTER TO COPYRIGHT OFFICE

Register of Copyrights
Library of Congress
Washington D.C. 20559

Gentlepersons:

Please conduct a search and tell me about registrations in any of the following names.

As a composer, I have used the names _____ and _____ and I have filed Form E and Form U and Form PA

As a publisher, I have used the names _____ and _____, and I have filed Form E and Form U and Form PA

It is possible that I may have claimed copyright as a publisher not only as _____ (for example, Room Seven Music), but also as _____ (for example, Room Seven Music Co, Room Seven Music Publishing, Room Seven Music Publishers, Room Seven)

I am sure that I did not write or register any song before 19_____. Therefore, you need search your files only for years after 19_____.

I (or a publisher named_____) also filed a claim for copyright in a songbook entitled _____. I was (or was not) the sole writer of the contents of the book. Please furnish registration data concerning the book, registered approximately 19____.

I have been informed that, pursuant to Section 708 (a) of the Copyright Act, your fee is $10. per hour for making and reporting of a search.

Enclosed is my check (or a money order) for $_____.

Please report to me before continuing the search once the fee is used up (OR: Please bill me for any extra fee).

Yours truly,

CHAPTER 30. REGISTRATION LETTER OF TRANSMITTAL.

Register of Copyrights
Library of Congress
Washington, D.C. 20559

Gentlepersons:

Enclosed is a PA Form and $10.00 registration fee for <u>each</u> of the following musical compositions:

COMPOSITION   *SONGWRITERS*

1.
2.
3.
4.

    Fee at $10.00 each times_____songs equals $_____
Check No._____
                                 Yours truly,

(NOTE: Be sure to keep a photocopy or carbon copy of the filled out portions of each Form attached to <u>your</u> copy of this letter. A copy of the letter of transmittal and (form is filed in the green label COPYRIGHT OFFICE - LETTERS To _____ (YEAR) file).

(NOTE: Frequently, publishers forget whether a particular song
registration form was sent to the Copyright Office. This
REGISTRATION LETTER OF TRANSMITTAL, if dated, and the
check No., can help the publisher remember when the
Form PA was sent to the Copyright Office.

CHAPTER 31. THE PUBLISHER'S GREEN LABEL COPYRIGHT OFFICE FILES

We have used radiant green labels for files concerning:

COPYRIGHT OFFICE

ASCAP
BMI
SESAC

SONG INDEX files.

The Copyright Office files include:

COPYRIGHT OFFICE	*-*	*Form*	*A*	*Registrations*
"	"	*-*	" *E*	"
"	"	*-*	" *U*	"
"	"	*-*	" *R*	"
"	"	*-*	" *PA*	"
"	"	*-*	" *TX*	"
"	"	*-*	" *RE*	"
"	"	*-*	*Letters To*	
"	"	*-*	*Letters From*	
"	"	*-*	*Do work*	

Other Copyright Office files

contain current blank forms and yet others contain circulars.

COPYRIGHT OFFICE	*-*	*Blank*	*Form*	*PA*
"	"	*-*	"	" *SR*
"	"	*-*	"	" *TX*
"	"	*-*	"	" *VA*
"	"	*-*	"	" *RE*
"	"	*-*	"	" *CA*
"	"	*-*	"	" *GR/cp*
"	"	*-*		" *IS*

The Copyright Office reaction to a request for forms is to send the forms. When they arrive, write on your copy of the letter requesting forms in the *LETTERS TO* file. "Forms were received on_____ "

That will enable you to use the original letter as a form for later, similar letters, and will enable you to calculate the approximate passage of time between a request for forms and the arrival of forms.

The Copyright Office reaction to a poorly completed Form PA or other attempted registration, generally, is to <u>keep</u> the forms and <u>send</u> a letter explaining the reason for not accepting the registration. When the forms are kept by the Copyright Office, the publisher can look at the photocopies attached to his letter of transmittal in the Copyright Office Letters To file.

The publisher, upon receipt of a rejection letter, should attach to it the original letter of transmittal and attached photocopies of original forms write across each rejected form's photocopy "REJECTED_____(date). These may be filed in the file, marked COPYRIGHT OFFICE - DO WORK, attached to the letter from the Copyright Office.

An attempt should be made to prepare corrected new forms immediately.

Prepare a new letter of transmittal. Attach the new forms behind the new letter of transmittal. Be sure to use the file identification number used by the Copyright Office. I like to attach a photocopy of the letter from the letter from the Copyright Office to the new letter of transmittal.

A copy of this package (letter of Transmittal, new forms, copy of letter from Copyright Office, is placed ahead of the relevant material in the COPYRIGHT OFFICE - DO WORK file. Since the work has been done, and the package mailed, a copy of everything is placed in the COPYRIGHT OFFICE-LETTERS TO FILE.

When the Copyright Office accepts forms for registration, it writes on the form the registration, number and date. The Copyright Office then returns the approved and registered forms to the publisher. This causes great joy.

The publisher should immediately photocopy each such approved form. File a photocopy in the respective pink label song file. File the returned form in the green label COPYRIGHT OFFICE-FORM PA REGISTRATIONS file.

Write on the copy of the letter of transmittal "Copyright Office returned the approved and registered forms on_____."

The letter of transmittal is left in the COPYRIGHT OFFICE - *LETTERS TO FILE*.

The publisher may, from time to time, as years end or as files become too thick, place date(s) on a closed *COPYRIGHT OFFICE-LETTERS TO- 1/1/Year 1 to 12/31/Year 3, and* open a new green label file: *COPYRIGHT OFFICE - LETTERS TO 1/1/Year 4-*.

An acco fastener may be used to securely tie the papers in the closed file to the file folder.

Before a file is closed, the publisher should remove any letters of transmittal and attached forms which have not been processed by the Copyright Office, and place them in the new *COPYRIGHT OFFICE-LETTERS TO FILE*.

The publisher may also place a photocopy of the registered
PA in other files:

SONGWRITER files of each songwriter.

PUBLISHER files of each publisher mentioned on the Form PA.

The color coordinated files have proven to aid a businessman
find important papers much more quickly.

CHAPTER 32.   THE PUBLISHER'S GREEN LABEL ASCAP FILES.

ASCAP'S files are somewhat similar to the Copyright Office file.

The general idea is to register songs written by ASCAP writers with ASCAP, and to be able to easily learn, at a later time, which songs have been registered.

    ASCAP - CONTRACT (Publisher) - YEAR
    ASCAP - CONTRACT (Composer) - YEAR

    ASCAP -   SMALL INDEX CARD REGISTRATIONS
    ASCAP -   SONG CLEARANCE FORM REGISTRATIONS

    ASCAP -   BLANK INDEX CARDS
    ASCAP -   BLANK SONG CLEARANCE FORMS.
    ASCAP -   PUBLICITY BOOKLETS
    ASCAP -   MAGAZINES

    ASCAP -   LETTERS TO
    ASCAP -   LETTERS FROM
    ASCAP -   DO WORK

Be sure to use a specifically dated letter of transmittal, whenever you send registration cards or clearance forms to ASCAP.   List every musical composition by title, authors and composers.

Attach a photocopy of each card or form sent to ASCAP to the letter of transmittal. On each photocopy write the date of the letter of transmittal.

Wait a month for ASCAP to respond. If ASCAP does respond, correct your registration forms.

If ASCAP does not respond, or acknowledges receipt of the registrations, then react accordingly to achieve the result that every SONG file shows that the song has been registered.

ALSO remove the index card or song clearance form from the LETTERS TO FILE and place them in the appropriate SMALL INDEX CARD REGISTRATIONS or SONG CLEARANCE FORM REGISTRATIONS FILE.

The small index cards may easily be alphabetized surrounded by rubber bands. You may wish to have a special index card size box for ASCAP index cards. We suggest that you have radiant green labels on all six sides of the box, each indicating in large letters "ASCAP INDEX CARD REGISTRATIONS."

CHAPTER 33. THE PUBLISHER'S GREEN LABEL BMI FILES

The pattern of BMI files recognizes, that there should be files for contracts, for blank forms, for pending letters, for accepted registrations.

> *BMI- CONTRACT (Publisher) - Year*
> *BMI- CONTRACT (Writer)   - Year*
>
> *BMI* - Songwriter's Clearance Form Registrations
> *BMI* - Publisher's Clearance Form Registrations.
>
> *BMI* - Blank Songwriter's Clearance forms
> *BMI* - Blank Publisher's Clearance forms.
> *BMI* - Blank other Forms.
> *BMI* - Publicity Booklets
> *BMI* - Magazine
>
> *BMI* - LETTERS TO
> *BMI* - LETTERS FROM
> *BMI* - DO WORK

The general idea is to register songs written by BMI writers with BMI.

Some publishers prepare clearance forms for <u>themselves and</u> also, for the same song, <u>their co-publishers and songwriters.</u> This may be done simply as a clerical matter, and can avoid later confusion concerning appropriate shares and possible financial loss to songwriters who fail to register their songs.

Forms should be sent to BMI with a dated letter of transmittal, which should set forth, in alphabetical order, the title of each song, the writers and any co-publishers.

A copy should be made of each form, and should be attached to a copy of the letter of transmittal (which shall be filed in the green label folder: BMI - LETTERS TO.)

BMI returns properly prepared song clearance forms, and indicates on such forms the date of receipt or indexing.

The publisher shall, if he receives a letter of transmittal from BMI, pull the publisher's letter of transmittal out of the BMI-LETTERS TO file, and refile everything in the BMI-LETTERS FROM file.

If there is no return letter of transmittal from BMI, the publisher shall write on his original letter of transmittal *"BMI indexed all songs on or about _____"*.

TITLE: **(DURATION IN MINUTES)**

LIST PRODUCTION/FILM TITLE IF ANY

COMPOSER (AFFILIATION)	AUTHOR (AFFILIATION)

CHECK	ORIGINAL COPYRIGHT		
ONE	ARR. OF PUBLIC DOMAIN WORK		ARR: (AFFILIATION)
COPYRIGHT OWNER			PUBLISHER (AFFILIATION)

MEMBER CONTROLLING PERFORMING RIGHTS IN THE U.S.A.

PERCENTAGE OF PUB. FEES CLAIMED:	DATE OF COPYRIGHT
	COPYRIGHT ENTRY NUMBER
	DO NOT WRITE IN THIS SPACE

IF ON ASSIGNMENT, PROVIDE COPY INDICATING EFFECTIVE DATE   58

Publisher Clearance Form

Broadcast Music, Inc., 40 West 57th Street, New York, N. Y. 10019

Att. Clearance/Logging Department

THIS FORM MUST BE FILLED OUT IN
ACCORDANCE WITH INSTRUCTIONS ON
THE REVERSE SIDE AND <u>BOTH COPIES</u>
<u>MUST BE RETURNED TO BMI.</u>

TLE – ONE WORK PER FORM

BASED ON PUBLIC DOMAIN – GIVE ORIGINAL TITLE AND SOURCE

HECK IF WORK IS FROM:
☐ MOTION PICTURE   GIVE TITLE OF FILM OR SHOW
☐ BROADWAY SHOW
☐ OFF-BROADWAY SHOW

	NT2 Credit Rate	Mulpt Credit	Clearance	BMI	Log	
					U.S.	Cand.
	NT3	Cand. Review	Clearance Is		Record	Lead Sheet

WRITER NAME(S)			WRITER ADDRESS(ES)	Perf. Rts. Orgn.	Share	Mode of Payment	WH
LAST	FIRST	MIDDLE					
C. SEC. NO.			-------------				
C. SEC. NO.			-------------				
C. SEC. NO.			-------------				
C. SEC. NO.			-------------				
C. SEC. NO.			-------------				
C. SEC. NO.			-------------				

PUBLISHER(S) IF WORK IS OF FOREIGN ORIGIN, GIVE NAME OF ORIGINAL PUBLISHER.	Perf. Rts. Orgn.	Share	Credit		WH	Orig. Pub.	World Rights	No Printin Bulletin
			U.S.	Cand.				
. ORIGINAL PUBLISHER(S):								
. SUB PUBLISHER: (PLEASE GIVE TERRITORIES)								
REIGN ORIGINAL PUBLISHER:								

NAME AND ADDRESS OF SUBMITTING PUBLISHER

AIL
ONFIRM-
ION
:

1ST RECORD RELEASE RECORD LABEL & NO.

ARTIST   RELEASE DATE

DATE SUBMITTED TO BMI

AUTHORIZED SIGNATURE

CLEARED IN ACCORDANCE WITH TERMS ON REVERSE SIDE

INSTRUCTIONS

PUBLISHER MUST COMPLETELY FILL OUT columns on left side of page and RETURN TO BMI CLEARANCE/LOGGING DEPARTMENT. <u>DO NOT</u> fill in columns on right side. <u>(BOTH COPIES OF THIS FORM MUST BE RETURNED TO BMI)</u>.

TITLE   Give complete title of work you are submitting for clearance. If also known under another title, please indicate a/k/a (also known as) and give other title. <u>(ONLY ONE WORK PER FORM)</u>.

- If this work is based on a Public Domain Work, GIVE ORIGINAL TITLE AND SOURCE. LEAD SHEET AND (OR) RECORDING <u>MUST BE SUBMITTED WITH CLEARANCE FORMS</u>.

                If this work was written for a Full Length Feature Motion Picture (NOT A FILM MADE FOR TV) or a Broadway or Off-Broadway Show, check appropriate box and give complete title of Motion Picture or Show.

WRITER(S)   Give complete name of each writer. If pseudonym, give complete name of writer under pseudonym. <u>Last Name first followed by First Name and Middle Name or Initial.</u> Give Social Security No. of each writer.

                Give name of PERFORMING RIGHTS ORGANIZATION (Perf. Rts. Orgn.) with which each writer is affiliated.

                Give share to which each writer is entitled. (ALL WRITERS' SHARES COMBINED SHOULD TOTAL 100%)

PUBLISHER(S)   Give complete name of each publisher.

                If you acquired this work from a publisher outside the United States, give complete name and address of the original publisher, territories and ATTACH AN ADDITIONAL COPY OF THIS FORM.

                Give name of PERFORMING RIGHTS ORGANIZATION (Perf. Rts. Orgn.) with which each publisher is affiliated.

                Give share to which each U.S. publisher is entitled. (ALL U.S. PUBLISHERS' SHARES COMBINED SHOULD TOTAL 100%).

RECORD   If this work has been recorded, give the record label and number, artist and date it was or will be released.

DATE   Give the date you are submitting this work to BMI.

SIGNATURE   This form must be signed by an authorized representative of the submitting publisher.

<u>IF ALL OF THE ABOVE INSTRUCTIONS ARE NOT FOLLOWED, THIS WORK WILL NOT BE REGISTERED FOR LOGGING PURPOSES AND THE FORM WILL BE RETURNED TO YOU FOR COMPLETION.</u>

CLEARANCE TERMS

THE RETURN OF A STAMPED COPY OF THIS FORM INDICATES THAT THE WORK LISTED ON THE REVERSE SIDE HAS BEEN CLEARED AND WILL BE ANNOUNCED IN OUR FORTHCOMING BULLETIN TO STATIONS.

Please note that in the event that a work cleared is published or recorded with lyrics which we, in our sole judgment, regard as unsuitable for broadcast use or with musical or lyrical material which we, in our sole judgment, regard as an infringement, we reserve the right at any time to exclude this work in its entirety from the provisions of our agreement and to withdraw the clearance.

We bring to your attention that in the event a clearance form submitted does not properly indicate in the space provided therefor that a work is based on public domain source, we reserve the right, if at any time such work is found to have a public domain source, to allocate to such work a percentage of the normal logging credit or, in the case of a work having little or no original material, to give no logging credit to such work.

Michael Tortora

Michael Tortora
Clearance - Logging Dept.

FORM PA

REGISTRATION NUMBER
PA   PAU

EFFECTIVE DATE OF REGISTRATION
. . . .
Month   Day   Year

DO NOT WRITE ABOVE THIS LINE. IF YOU NEED MORE SPACE, USE CONTINUATION SHEET (FORM PA/CON)

(1) Title

TITLE OF THIS WORK:

NATURE OF THIS WORK:
(See instructions)

PREVIOUS OR ALTERNATIVE TITLES:

(2) Author(s)

IMPORTANT: Under the law, the "author" of a "work made for hire" is generally the employer, not the employee (see instructions). If any part of this work was "made for hire" check "Yes" in the space provided, give the employer (or other person for whom the work was prepared) as "Author" of that part, and leave the space for dates blank.

1

NAME OF AUTHOR:

Was this author's contribution to the work a "work made for hire"?   Yes......   No......

DATES OF BIRTH AND DEATH:
Born .... Died ....
(Year)   (Year)

AUTHOR'S NATIONALITY OR DOMICILE:
Citizen of .... } or { Domiciled in ....
(Name of Country)   (Name of Country)

WAS THIS AUTHOR'S CONTRIBUTION TO THE WORK:
Anonymous?   Yes.......   No.......
Pseudonymous?   Yes.......   No.......

AUTHOR OF: (Briefly describe nature of this author's contribution)

If the answer to either of these questions is "Yes," see detailed instructions attached.

2

NAME OF AUTHOR:

Was this author's contribution to the work a "work made for hire"?   Yes......   No......

DATES OF BIRTH AND DEATH:
Born .... Died ....
(Year)   (Year)

AUTHOR'S NATIONALITY OR DOMICILE:
Citizen of .... } or { Domiciled in ....
(Name of Country)   (Name of Country)

WAS THIS AUTHOR'S CONTRIBUTION TO THE WORK:
Anonymous?   Yes.......   No.......
Pseudonymous?   Yes.......   No.......

AUTHOR OF: (Briefly describe nature of this author's contribution)

If the answer to either of these questions is "Yes," see detailed instructions attached.

3

NAME OF AUTHOR:

Was this author's contribution to the work a "work made for hire"?   Yes......   No......

DATES OF BIRTH AND DEATH:
Born .... Died ....
(Year)   (Year)

AUTHOR'S NATIONALITY OR DOMICILE:
Citizen of .... } or { Domiciled in ....
(Name of Country)   (Name of Country)

WAS THIS AUTHOR'S CONTRIBUTION TO THE WORK:
Anonymous?   Yes.......   No.......
Pseudonymous?   Yes.......   No.......

AUTHOR OF: (Briefly describe nature of this author's contribution)

If the answer to either of these questions is "Yes," see detailed instructions attached.

(3) Creation and Publication

YEAR IN WHICH CREATION OF THIS WORK WAS COMPLETED:

Year..........

(This information must be given in all cases.)

DATE AND NATION OF FIRST PUBLICATION:

Date. . . . .
(Month)   (Day)   (Year)

Nation . . . .
(Name of Country)

(Complete this block ONLY if this work has been published.)

(4) Claimant(s)

NAME(S) AND ADDRESS(ES) OF COPYRIGHT CLAIMANT(S):

TRANSFER: (If the copyright claimant(s) named here in space 4 are different from the author(s) named in space 2, give a brief statement of how the claimant(s) obtained ownership of the copyright.)

Complete all applicable spaces (numbers 5-9) on the reverse side of this page.
Follow detailed instructions attached.
Sign the form at line 8.

DO NOT WRITE HERE
Page 1 of .... pages

61.

DO NOT WRITE ABOVE THIS LINE. IF YOU NEED ADDITIONAL SPACE, USE CONTINUATION SHEET (FORM PA/CON)

PREVIOUS REGISTRATION:

- Has registration for this work, or for an earlier version of this work, already been made in the Copyright Office? Yes . . . . No . . . .

- If your answer is "Yes," why is another registration being sought? (Check appropriate box)

  ☐ This is the first published edition of a work previously registered in unpublished form.
  ☐ This is the first application submitted by this author as copyright claimant.
  ☐ This is a changed version of the work, as shown by line 6 of the application.

- If your answer is "Yes," give: Previous Registration Number . . . . Year of Registration . . . .

⑤ Previous Registration

COMPILATION OR DERIVATIVE WORK: (See instructions)

PREEXISTING MATERIAL: (Identify any preexisting work or works that the work is based on or incorporates.)

. . . .
. . . .
. . . .
. . . .

MATERIAL ADDED TO THIS WORK: (Give a brief, general statement of the material that has been added to this work and in which copyright is claimed.)

. . . .
. . . .
. . . .
. . . .

⑥ Compilation or Derivative Work

DEPOSIT ACCOUNT: (If the registration fee is to be charged to a Deposit Account established in the Copyright Office, give name and number of Account.)

Name: . . . .

Account Number: . . . .

CORRESPONDENCE: (Give name and address to which correspondence about this application should be sent.)

Name: . . . .

Address: . . . . (Apt.)

. . . .
(City)　　　　　　　　(State)　　　　　　　　(ZIP)

⑦ Fee and Correspondence

CERTIFICATION: ✱ I, the undersigned, hereby certify that I am the: (Check one)

☐ author ☐ other copyright claimant ☐ owner of exclusive right(s) ☐ authorized agent of: . . . .
(Name of author or other copyright claimant, or owner of exclusive right(s))

of the work identified in this application and that the statements made by me in this application are correct to the best of my knowledge.

☞ Handwritten signature: (X) . . . .

Typed or printed name. . . . . Date . . . .

⑧ Certification (Application must be signed)

MAIL CERTIFICATE TO

. . . .
(Name)

. . . .
(Number, Street and Apartment Number)

. . . .
(City)　　　　(State)　　　　(ZIP code)

(Certificate will be mailed in window envelope)

⑨ Address For Return of Certificate

✱ 17 U.S.C. §506(e) FALSE REPRESENTATION—Any person who knowingly makes a false representation of a material fact in the application for copyright registration provided for by ¢ section 409. or in any written statement filed in connection with the application, shall be fined not more than $2,500.

Nov. 1977 - 1,000,0

The MUSIC INDUSTRY
As Seen by a PUBLISHER

64.

RECORDING STUDIO

YOUR DEMO TAPE IS OKAY BUT I'LL TRY TO HAVE A BETTER ONE MADE. I WANT TO GIVE YOUR SONG EVERY POSSIBLE CHANCE!

THE PUBLISHER'S WORK BEGINS...

"THEN I'LL HAVE COPIES MADE ON TAPES AND DISCS."

"I'LL PLAY THE DEMO TO POTENTIAL USERS..IN MY OFFICE... IN THEIR OFFICES ...WHEREVER I CAN CATCH THEM."

"I'LL ALSO MAIL COPIES TO POTENTIAL USERS— ARTISTS, RECORD COMPANIES, MOVIE PRODUCERS, ETC.!"

103

"But that's only the beginning of my work, Mr. Songwriter. Next, I'll have a clear and professional lead sheet made up on 8 1/2" by 11" paper."

"Then I'll put a copyright notice on the bottom of the sheet...Like this..."

© MCMLXXXI Suite·Seven Music (ASCAP)

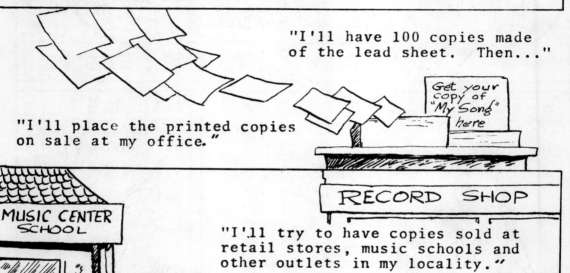

"I'll have 100 copies made of the lead sheet. Then..."

"I'll place the printed copies on sale at my office."

"I'll try to have copies sold at retail stores, music schools and other outlets in my locality."

"I'll send copies to people who may record the song."

"I'll also keep copies in my car and in my brief case so I can show them to interested people."

66.

106

68.

69.

"I will license Recording Companies, Television Producers and others to use the song..."

MR. RECORDING CO., I AUTHORIZE YOU TO MAKE A RECORD MASTER OF MY SONG.

FINE!

The license to record a song as a phonograph record master is usually oral, and usually no fee is paid.

MR. RECORD CO., I HEREBY AUTHORIZE YOU TO USE MY SONG ON PHONOGRAPH RECORDS

AND I HEREBY PROMISE TO PAY YOU ROYALTIES ON ALL RECORDS SOLD.

MECHANICAL LICENSE

MS. T.V. PRODUCER, I HEREBY AUTHORIZE YOU TO HAVE MY SONG PERFORMED ON YOUR T.V. SHOW

AND I PROMISE TO PAY YOU A FEE FOR THIS USE OF YOUR SONG.

TELEVISION LICENSE

108

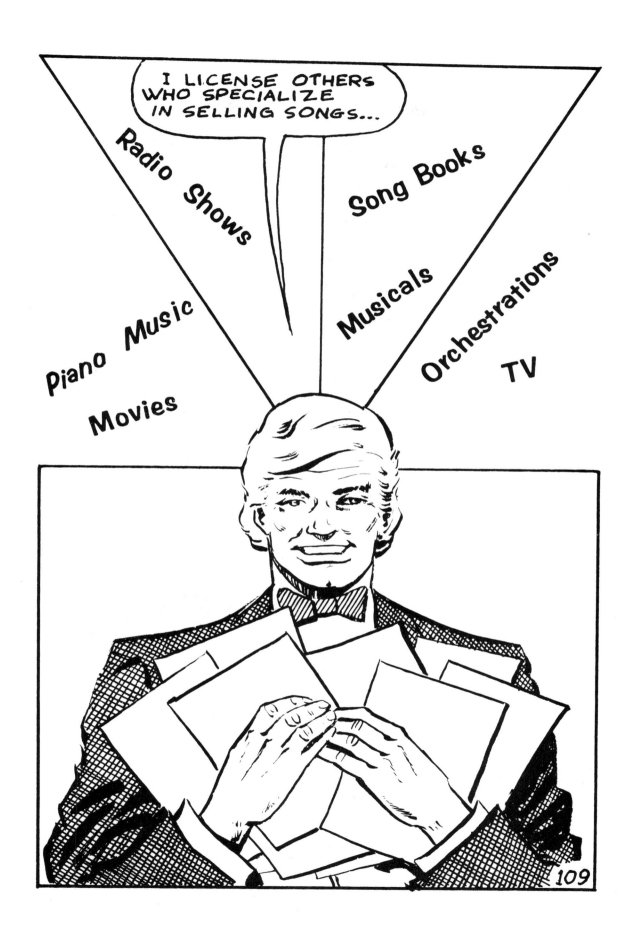

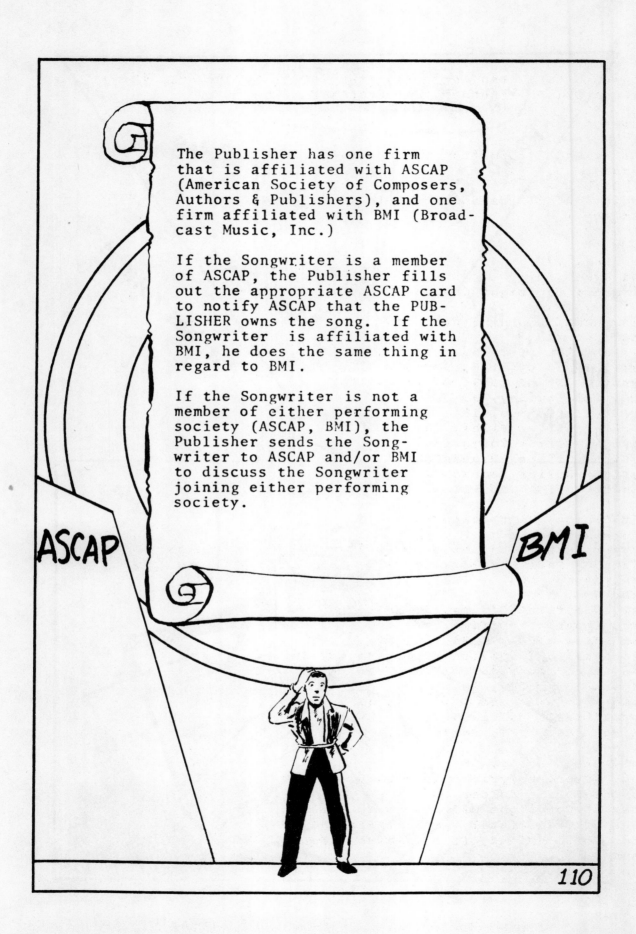

The Publisher has one firm that is affiliated with ASCAP (American Society of Composers, Authors & Publishers), and one firm affiliated with BMI (Broadcast Music, Inc.)

If the Songwriter is a member of ASCAP, the Publisher fills out the appropriate ASCAP card to notify ASCAP that the PUBLISHER owns the song. If the Songwriter is affiliated with BMI, he does the same thing in regard to BMI.

If the Songwriter is not a member of either performing society (ASCAP, BMI), the Publisher sends the Songwriter to ASCAP and/or BMI to discuss the Songwriter joining either performing society.

ASCAP

BMI

110

AFTRA, 10.
Alpha-Numeric System For Classification of Recordings, 42.
American Guild of Authors and Composers, 10.
ANSCR, 42.
ASCAP, 20
ASCAP Files, 56.
ASCAP Record Information Sheet, 44.
Assignee, 10.
Assignor, 10.
Association of Independent Music Publishers, 10.
Backstage, 10.
Billboard, 10.
BMI, 20.
BMI Files, 57.
Brand Name, 14.
California Copyright Conference, 10.
Cash Box, 10.
College For Recording Arts, 10.
Contracts, 12.
Copyright Act of 1976, Section 101, 7.
Copyright Act of 1976, Section 115, 19.
Copyright Act of 1909, 2¢ Rate, 18.
Commercial Quality, 9.
Compulsory License, 18.
Copyright Office Files, 53.
Copyright Office Forms, 48.
Copyright Office, Request Letter, 50.
Copyright Office, Search Letter, 51.
Costs of Copies and Files, 46.
Demo, 9.
Don't Overpay Your Songwriter, 33.
Employees, 26.
Employer Identification Number, 25.
Fictitious Name Certificate, 23.
Files, Ascap, 56.
Files, BMI, 57.
Files, Copyright Office, 53.
Forms, Copyright Office, 48.
Green Label Ascap Files, 56, 58,
Green Label BMI Publishers Clearance, 59, 60.
Green Label Copyright Office Form PA, 61, 62.
Hollywood Reporter, 10.
Income From Hits and Non-Hits, 47.
International Musician, 10.
Joining Ascap, BMI, Sesac, 22.
Knowledge, 16.
Label, Green Ascap, 56.
Label, Green, Copyright Office, 53.
Lead Sheet file folder, 41
Letter to Copyright Office, Forms Request, 50.
Letter of Transmittal, Registration, 52.
Letter To Copyright Office, Search Request, 51.
Licensee, 10.
Licensor, 10.
Lyric Sheet, 3.
Master, 9.
Money, 8.

Overture, 10.
Payroll Problems & Procedures, 27.
Pink Label File Folder, 39.
Publisher's Copyright Office Files, 53.
Publisher's Green Label ASCAP Files, 56.
Notice of Intention to Obtain Compulsory License, 19
Publisher's Green Label BMI Files, 57
Publisher's Green Label Copyright Office Files, 53
Publisher Is In The Money Business, 35.
Radio and Records, 10.
Receipt, 34
Record World, 10.
Registration Letter of Transmittal, 52.
Request Letter to Copyright Office, 50.
Search Letter to Copyright Office, 51.
SESAC, 52
Song Index Files, 47.
Song Paperwork Checklist, 40
Sound Recordings and Printed Matter, 40.
Song Pink Label File Folder 39.
Songwriter's Information Sheet, 30.
Songwriter's List of Songs, 31.
Songwriter - Needed Information, 29.
Songwriter's Royalty Summary, 32.
Talent, 3.
Time, 5.
Two point seventy-five cents per song, 19.
Uncle Sam is in the Taxing Business, 37.
United States Employer Identification Number, 25.
Variety, 10.

OFFICIAL JOURNAL **Overture**

DON MORRIS, Editor

MUSICIANS MUTUAL PROTECTIVE ASSN., LOCAL 47, A. F. of M.
817 N. VINE STREET, LOS ANGELES 38, CALIF.

THE RECORDING INDUSTRY

By Rene J. Hall

In my over thirty years as sideman, leader, aranger, recording consultant, independent master producer, and now member of the Board of Directors of Local 47, I have often wished that our field had a reference book which could answer our questions—just as electricians and engineers and various mechanics have reference books in their fields to supply answers to their professional problems.

Quite recently, I was presented with a copy of such a book, written by an attorney friend of mine who is an expert in the field of recordings. He knows what makes it tick, and quotes book, chapter and verse in one big volume.

Having found this book to be of invaluable assistance to me in the field of independent master producing, I would like to take this opportunity to recommend it to the many musicians, who, like myself, are either already in or are desirous of entering this particular field of endeavor.

Everything is covered here, from fascinating case histories of artists, publishers, and songs, to the financing, big and small, of record companies, record sessions and independent record productions; how they are started and run. The book is packed, too, with explanatory charts and illustrations, sample contracts dealing with musicians, artists, distributors, etc., etc., etc., including foreign rights.

Although the cost of this book is less than one-half of a record date, it will both make and save a lot of money for anyone armed with its vast store of business knowledge. A musician may suggest to the owners of the clubs in which he plays or to his regular employers, that they finance master producing sessions at scale for playing and arranging, and thus have a chance at record exposure and royalties.

In my honest opinion this book is a real must for anyone engaged in or thinking of entering the business, a book that you will not only read with interest but that you will keep for research and answers that come up.

In the course of conduct of my daily business, I'm asked many questions by both beginners and professionals of many years standing, the answers to which were to be found within the pages of his highly informative book.

I wish that I could have had this book thirty years ago. Now, I have one copy of the book at home for reading and one available at my office for reference.

Walter E. Hurst writes with scholarly knowledge; w . . compassion for people in the industry, with wit and good humor and sugar-coats the lessons that we must all learn.

There are many of us in he business who would have saved much work, money, and heartbreak if they had had, "THE RECORD INDUSTRY" (How to Make Money In the Record Industry) by Walter E. Hurst, published by 7 Arts Press, 1775 Las Palmas, Hollywood 28, California. ($25.00); to guide them.

NEW BOOKS

The complex and highly competitive recording business is given an exhaustive treatment by Walter E. Hurst, Hollywood attorney and advocate-at-law who has specilized in this field, and William Storm Hale (a non de plume to protect his identity) in a book tentatively titled "The Record Industry" ("How to Make Money In the Record Industry"), to be published by 7 Arts Press of Hollywood next month at $25 a copy. It's a big book, covering all angles and operations from songwriter, singer, publisher and disc firm down to the retail store; going into detail about contracts, distribution and promotion; citing artists who have made money; telling what artists should know about personal managers, disc jockeys, payola, the music trade press; the law of the recording field, Congressional investigation, etc. All in all, the book presents an almost overwhelming array of information, sprinkled with illustrations, charts and tabulations, sample forms, etc., that should prove invaluable to anyone in the record business or planning to enter the field.

•

NIGHT LIFE IN CHICAGO

Sid Ascher

THE RECORD INDUSTRY BOOK: Just finished reading a most fascinating book—"The Record Industry Book" (How To Make Money in The Record Industry) Volume One. This to me is truly wonderful. If you are already in the record business; if you want to go into the business; if you are a song writer or publisher, or a recording artist, this book is "must" reading. It is really an encyclopedia of the recording industry and should be in every library in the nation.

DAILY *VARIETY* DAILY

WHAT'S THE SCORE?

By JOHN G. HOUSER

★ ★ ★

WORDS AND MUSIC: "THE RECORD INDUSTRY." AUTHORS Walter E. Hurst and William Storm Hale have contributed a massive, monumental and authoritative work that is as comprehensive a study of an intricate industry as it is possible to reveal. The material included in the invaluable work is a compendium and a textbook for neophyte and journeyman in all facets of the disk biz. It will be classed (as is Blackstone and Gray's Anatomy in the legal and medical professions) as the supreme authority for those in the recording industry. The price, $25, will be an investment many times recovered if the purchaser makes use of the lessons to be learned (the easy way). Authors have made "the lessons" an exciting panorama of case histories from artist to copyright and promotion to payola. Published by 7 Arts Press, the book should be at the right hand of every a&r man, musician, songwriter and publisher . . .

CALIFORNIA TOWN & COUNTRY

NOVEMBER-DECEMBER--1971

BOOK REVIEW
BY CAROLINE HALL
THE MANAGERS, ENTERTAINER AND AGENTS BOOK
JOHNNY MINUS & WILLIAM STORM HALE

I have spent a quarter of a century as an entertainer, agent, booking agent, talent scouting and as a manager and last but not least as a personal manager. I have worked with many managers, entertainers agents, lawyers, promoters songwriters, publishers and others in show business, some I have also worked against. I have booked many stars and aspiring stars. I have lenared one thing-show business brings out the best or the worst in a person, but it allows both stars and associates an exciting and full life. Most young people, who read fan magazine and day-dream about themselves as a great singer, actor, singer, performer and all the glamor is there so they start out in a neighborhood or school event to become the leading lady or man. Sometimes fond parents cheer them on or force them, encourage their offsprings, but only until the point when the parents worry about the horrible temptations and dangers that they face when they enter show business. The parents are afraid that they will become bums with a unpredictable future. There are books and courses for youngsters who want to prepare themselves for any number of careers. There has never been a book written that will guarantee you success, but this book THE ENTERTAINEMTN INDUSTRY SERIES, AND THE MANAGER'S, ENTERTAINERS and AGENTS BOOK is probably the best guideline for you to follow. If you were an entertainer and are looking for a manager to manage your career and a stranger told you that he was a manager and would like to manage you how would you qualify him. If you wanted to be or were a manager or agent, and a singer, songwriter, group and a performer wanted you to manage them how would you qualify the performer, etc. I have not had the book available to me, but THE MANAGERS', ENTERTAINERS' and AGENTS BOOK, I am glad that the book exist, however, if you do purchase this book for fun, profit and help to guide you in your career remember one thing it is a guide and do not for one minute buy it for instant success, but use it as a reference and a guide and it will help you in the business of the STARS, SHOW PEOPLE and the people around them. You also will probably reap the harvest that is there.

Thursday, October 21, 1971

Hollywood Guide Gives
What Newcomers Need

By TOM DOYLE

It should have been titled "Something for Everyone" or "The Ridding of the Green"; it should have been printed by a guy who didn't leave his glasses home that day, and, it could have been half its size (and weight) if someone hadn't been addicted to double spacing and poor chapter construction.

Still, it is one whale of a book and should be required reading for everyone in (or who would like to be in) the entertainment business.

"It" is "THE MANAGERS,' ENTERTAINERS' AND AGENTS' BOOK" by Johnny Minus and William Storm Hale (pseudonyms) (7 Arts Press, $35.00). I propose the above title changes because the authors have omitted no phase of the industry in their often devastating analyses and

because of their sincere (although they would prefer you considered them hardened cynics) concern for those starry-eyed, alarmingly "green" newcomers, who arrive in this town with an overabundance of enthusiasm and a frighten ing absence of experience.

Throughout the book, wondered which provoked th authors — love or contempt:- to dedicate so much time t research and interviews for cure to a "condition" which has heretofore been accepte as "the nature of the beast." concluded it was both: A lov for the business and a wi ingness to improve it; and, "contempt for the laziness people who would rather was living expenses and time the school of hard knocks exercising their reading abili and time in order to impro the way they will spend t hours of their lives."

Some critics may find fa with the authors for offer what could be classified guidance for the naive (" best relationship is one respect") or for stating the vious ("show business rough, tough, rotten and dis pointing"). I could not ag with these critics. I would stead ask: "Naive or obvi to whom?" The authors h taken nothing for granted they should be commended overcoming the temptatior do so.

Friday, December 17, 1971

THE Hollywood REPORTER

The Managers, Entertainers, Agents Book; Johnny Minus and W liam Storm Hale; Seven Arts Pr $35.

In "The Managers, Entertair and Agents Book," the sixth and la volume to join the Seven Arts P Entertainment Industry Series, aut Johnny Minus and William Storm H (pseudonyms) provide thorough cc age on—to borrow their subtit "how to plan, plot, scheme, le perform, avoid dangers, and enjoy career in the entertainment indus Using typewriter-script text, m duplications of contracts and re forms and applications, and cart strip illustrations of legal cases, 732-page compilation of guide includes almost all situations would affect the trio of the title. examination and exposé of bus "insides" — rarely available to and civilian, and the probable re for the pseudonymous authorshi makes this unique, local public a sound investment, worthy of the price tag, and a definite must for needing solid and accurate "How information on these occupatione visions of the business.

TO: SEVEN ARTS PRESS, INC. — Dept. AF

6605 Hollywood Boulevard, Suite 215, Hollywood, CA 90028

Please send me:

The MANAGERS', ENTERTAINERS' & AGENTS' BOOK

$35.00

_____

Enclosed is my check in the amount of $_____

NAME: _____

INSTITUTION: _____

ADDRESS: _____

CITY, STATE, ZIP _____

The World Beyond the Turntable

By Louis Chapin

The writing, promoting, recording, and publishing of popular songs is usually estimated in one of three ways. Either it is (a) something any fool can make a mint of money out of, or (b) something only a fool would risk his shirt in, or (c) well worth considering. The authors of **"The Record Industry Book, Volume One (How to Make Money in the Record Industry)"** are given, naturally, to opinion (c); yet they have written it so as at least to entertain, if not convert, the adherents of the other opinions.

These two authors are Walter E. Hurst and William Storm Hale—the former a lawyer and the latter apparently a figure of some prominence disguised by a pen name. Their bulky book has been published by Seven Arts Press in Hollywood in letter-size monolith at $25. In spite of unpromising typography, "The Record Industry Book" is written with a conversational style that almost reads itself.

Practical Guide

It is specifically informative, with a sprinkling of tables, charts, diagrams, comic-strip expositions, and sample documents (such as contracts and copyright forms). It should be a thoroughly practical guide to those concerned with the writing, playing, recording, publishing, selling, and otherwise exploiting of popular music. It might encourage the timid, and temper the overconfident.

Moreover, leavened as it is with free-wheeling anecdotal illustrations, "The Record Industry" may well be read and enjoyed by some who merely listen—and make the whole business possible. They will find breezy, conversational stretches of Americana, as "case histories" are leafed through, with both actual and fictitious names to document the rough and smooth sides of the pop music coin. They will find a busy, palpitating, apparently self-sufficient world of downbeats, takes, and royalties.

Pennies Add Up

They may be surprised, too, to learn of the tremendous volume on which record profits are predicated. The "artist" may realize only three or four cents a record, but when sales are "snowballed" up to 500,000 or 1,000,000 he'll need something bigger than a penny bank. And he may need to learn how to give his copyrights to charity, so that he can take home three times as much after taxes.

There are certain questions the reader will not find discussed in "The Record Industry." Among them: whether the whole operation represents the greatness of American enterprise with a song on its lips, or (conceivably) a colossal cultural short circuit. Or both.

Another question: whether the writing, performing, recording, and publishing of symphonies, operas, and other such "long-hair" items should be excluded from "the record industry" by definition. A front-page story in a recent Wall Street Journal was headlined "Opera Recordings Sell Briskly. . . . Birgit Nilsson's Turandot Outsells Hit Crosby Album." Apparently those other songwriters Mozart, Verdi, Puccini — even Kurt Weill — had some profitable skills.

It is significant, of course, that most of these booming opera records are made outside the United States, in countries where musicians' costs are still invitingly low. But where such a domestic market obviously exists, what enterprising man of industry is going to turn his back on possibilities (however remote) of domestic production?

"The Record Industry," it appears, is a thought-provoking book. And since a new and larger edition is already being contemplated, its authors may still take the opportunity of reconsidering their terms. And judging by the book in hand, they will do so good-naturedly and readably.

THE HOLLYWOOD REPORTER

The Managers, Entertainers, and Agents Book; Johnny Minus and William Storm Hale; Seven Arts Press, $35.

In "The Managers, Entertainers, and Agents Book," the sixth and latest volume to join the Seven Arts Press Entertainment Industry Series, authors Johnny Minus and William Storm Hale (pseudonyms) provide thorough coverage on—to borrow their subtitle—"how to plan, plot, scheme, learn, perform, avoid dangers, and enjoy your career in the entertainment industry." Using typewriter-script text, many duplications of contracts and related forms and applications, and cartoon-strip illustrations of legal cases, this 732-page compilation of guidelines includes almost all situations that would affect the trio of the title. The examination and exposé of business "insides" — rarely available to tyro and civilian, and the probable reason for the pseudonymous authorship — makes this unique, local publication a sound investment, worthy of the $35 price tag, and a definite must for those needing solid and accurate "How To-" information on these occupational divisions of the business.

★ ★ ★

WORDS AND MUSIC: "THE RECORD INDUSTRY." AUTHORS Walter E. Hurst and William Storm Hale have contributed a massive, monumental and authoritative work that is as comprehensive a study of an intricate industry as it is possible to reveal. The material included in the invaluable work is a compendium and a textbook for neophyte and journeyman in all facets of the disk biz. It will be classed (as is Blackstone and Gray's Anatomy in the legal and medical professions) as the supreme authority for those in the recording industry. The price, $25, will be an investment many times recovered if the purchaser makes use of the lessons to be learned (the easy way). Authors have made "the lessons" an exciting panorama of case histories from artist to copyright and promotion to payola. Published by 7 Arts Press, the book should be at the right hand of every a&r man, musician, songwriter and publisher . . .

WHAT'S THE SCORE?

By JOHN G. HOUSER

MOTION PICTURE DISTRIBUTION: (BUSINESS AND/OR RACKET?!?), by Walter E. Hurst and William Storm Hale. Seven Arts Press, Hollywood, CA; 1975; $10.00 paper; 158 pp.; illus.; index; biblio. What every film producer always wanted to know about distribution but was afraid to ask. Detailed handbook covers a wide variety of producer-distributor-exhibitor conflicts.

Educational Film Library
Association, Inc.

Browsing the Book Stalls ●

HOW TO BE A MUSIC PUBLISHER; by Walter E. Hurst & Don Rico; Seven Arts Press Inc.; 125 pages (paperback); $10.

The authors, a top Hollywood music attorney and a leading artist/illustrator and writer, have collaborated to produce a primer which covers the main principles of the music publishing business for songwriters, artists, musicians, distributors, teachers, students, accountants, attorneys, publicists and anyone else seeking to understand the rudiments of this multimillion-dollar industry.

While it is by no means a comprehensive guide to this end of the music business (and anyone seeking to enter it would be well advised to use this book merely as a point of departure for further research), nevertheless it does manage to provide a good overflow of the fundamentals which must be mastered.

It covers some of the basics of copyright law, contracts, licensing agreements, acquiring and selling song rights, etc. It also covers key principles of musical composition. It is an excellent companion volume to Hurst's earlier work (with William Storm Hale): "Introduction to Music/Record Copyright, Contracts and Other Business and Law."

There is much to learn about the business and legal aspects of the music and record industry — and this book is a welcome addition to available books on these subjects. **— John Charnay**

Entertainment Law

THE U.S. MASTER PRODUCERS & BRITISH MUSIC SCENE BOOK. By Walter E. Hurst and William Strom Hale. Hollywood: 7 Arts Press, 1968. Pp. 373. $25. Written by a lawyer working in the music and recording business, this book deals with the legal problems of record promotion, business and money promotion, recording contracts, and advertising. In addition, it includes sample contracts for all phases of dealings among artists, master producers, recording companies, fan clubs, record clubs, motion picture producers, talent scouts, music publishers, and television producers. Special attention is given to description of the music industry in England. Excerpts from British law books, the Performing Right Society Limited publications, and other trade publications are presented to inform the American artist or producer of his business rights in England and generally to acquaint him with the British industry. The book is thorough in its coverage and the table of contents and index are well designed.

`...` *SOUTHERN CALIFORNIA LAW REVIEW*

CALIFORNIA WESTERN LAW REVIEW

MOTION PICTURE DISTRIBUTION. By Walter E. Hurst and William Storm Hale. Seven Arts Press: Hollywood. 1974. Pp. 158. $10.00. The authors have prepared an easy to read review of the various aspects of motion picture distribution; its theory and practice. Various problem areas and pitfalls, as well as basic aspects of the subject area, are set forth in alphabetical sequence for easy reference and are intricately detailed through the use of definitional statements and practical forms and examples.

RE: THE PUBLISHERS OFFICE MANUAL

By WALTER E. HURST & WILLIAM STORM HALE

WHOEVER EXPECTED A TWENTY-FIVE DOLLAR (MUSIC) PUBLISHERS OFFICE MANUAL TO SELL TO SMALL LIBRARIES?

SEVEN ARTS PRESS, DID.   Here's why:

"IT IS THE ONLY BOOK OF ITS KIND"

She was 18 years old when her uncle helped her get a job in an office which prepared letters for songwriters and publishers to other (1) songwriters, (2) publishers, (3) record companies, (4) performance rights societies, (5) Copyright Office, (6) etc.

An office manual was written for her, and since she did not like to read, (she loved music) it was written with cartoons, dialog, baloons, wise-cracks, flow arrows, diagrams, numbered paper, capitals, italics, sample letters, simple royalty computations.

There is ample substance in this (music) publishers office manual for those who want it — files, bookeeping, taxes, analysis of an exclusive songwriters contract, ASCAP and BMI forms, Copyright Office circulars.

RECORD WORLD wrote: "*PUBLISHERS MANUAL INDISPENSABLE.*"   VARIETY wrote, "*A do-it-yourself tome for aspiring publishers has been compiled by Walter E. Hurst and William Storm Hale . . . Hip to all the contemporary music biz angles, Hurst & Hale even give instructions on how to handle a cut-in proposal . . .*"

The LIBRARY JOURNAL wrote: "*The weighty tome . . . pearls of wisdom . . . stories . . . special language . . . forms for contracts, copyrights, publishers clearance forms, and so on.*"

"The field of music publishing is one in which you might make over $50,000 by publishing a hit song. You might also lose the same $50,000 if you failed to file a Form U."
Extract from THE PUBLISHERS OFFICE MANUAL.

LIBRARIANS   — Give the Library's users an opportunity to benefit from reading this book, "IT IS THE ONLY BOOK OF ITS KIND."

— —

SEVEN ARTS PRESS, INC.
6605 Hollywood Blvd., No. 215, Hollywood, California 90028

Please send us for $25.00 each (5% Sales Tax for California residents)
———— copies of THE PUBLISHERS OFFICE MANUAL.

NAME: _____

ADDRESS: _____

CITY, STATE, ZIP: _____

SEVEN ARTS PRESS, INC.
P.O. Box 649
HOLLYWOOD, CALIFORNIA 90028

ASK YOUR FAVORITE BOOK STORE OR DISTRIBUTOR FOR OTHER VOLUMES OF
THE ENTERTAINMENT INDUSTRY SERIES

			PRICE
Vol. 1	The Record Industry Book (7th Edition)	Hardcover	$15.00
		Softcover	$10.00
Vol. 2	The Music Industry Book	Hardcover	$25.00
Vol. 3	The Publisher's Office Manual	Hardcover	$25.00
Vol. 4	The U.S. Master Producer's & British Music Scene Book	Hardcover	$25.00
Vol. 5	The Movie Industry Book	Hardcover	$35.00
Vol. 6	The Managers', Entertainers', and Agents' Book	Hardcover	$35.00
Vol. 7	Film--TV Law	Hardcover	$15.00
		Softcover	$10.00
Vol. 8	Films Superlist: 20,000 Films in the U.S. Public Domain	Hardcover	$95.00
	Ten Booklets in	Softcover	$59.50
Vol. 9	Music/Record Business & Law	Hardcover	$15.00
		Softcover	$10.00
Vol. 10	Motion Picture Distribution	Hardcover	$15.00
		Softcover	$10.00
Vol. 11	How To Be A Music Publisher (2nd Edition)	Hardcover	$15.00
		Softcover	$10.00
Vol. 12	Mr. Information Battles For The Taxpayer (Your Income Tax Comic Book)	Softcover	$10.00
Vol. 13	How To Start A Record Or Independent Production Company	Hardcover	$15.00
		Softcover	$10.00
Vol. 14	How To Register A Trademark	Hardcover	$15.00
		Softcover	$10.00
Vol. 15	Copyright (How To Register & Introduction To Historical & New Coypright)	Hardcover	$15.00
		Softcover	$10.00
Vol. 16	Copyright Registration Forms PA & SR	Hardcover	$15.00
		Softcover	$10.00

THIS BOOK: HARDCOVER ISBN 0-911370-35-8 $15.00
*   SOFTCOVER ISBN 0-911370-36-6 $10.00*